STORIES BY HAITIAN-AMERICAN TEENS

D1596130

By Youth Communication

Edited by Dana K. Vincent

True Stories by Teens

HAITI ON MY MIND

Executive Editors
Keith Hefner and Laura Longhine

Contributing Editors
Marie Glancy, Hope Vanderberg, Al Desetta,
Rachel Blustain, Clarence Haynes, Katia Hetter,
Andrea Estepa, Nora McCarthy, and Donna Wolff

Layout & Design
Efrain Reyes, Jr.

Cover Photograph
Tony Savino
www.tonysavino.com

For reprint information, please contact Youth Communication.

ISBN 978-1-935552-47-5

First Edition
Printed in the United States of America

Youth Communication ®
New York, New York
212-279-0708
www.youthcomm.org

TABLE OF CONTENTS

CONTENTS

FOREWORD

On January 12, 2010, a devastating earthquake all but leveled Haiti's capital and the surrounding areas. Amid the more than 300,000 who perished, survivors remain huddled by the thousands in refugee camps, most shielding themselves from intermittent rain with nothing but wooden posts and bed sheets.

How much more can Haiti bear? Even before the earthquake, adults in this country of nearly ten million were expected to live an average of 59 years if they are men, 60 if they are women. One out of five children died before their fifth birthday. The risk of dying from an infectious disease was always high; however, it has been exponentially increased by unsanitary living conditions since the earthquake.

The tally of Haiti's losses from the earthquake is now beyond measure. In a country where two-thirds of the population previously lacked formal employment, a large percentage of those who were employed were wiped out in the government buildings, hospitals, hotels, banks, supermarkets, and hundreds of other places where they were wrapping up their day. And the students, the young people. No one will ever really know how many of them died in after school tutoring sessions and university classrooms. The forty-five seconds the earthquake lasted produced an instant brain drain for Haiti, followed by yet another exodus that the country can ill afford.

During my first trip to Haiti after the earthquake, I was amazed to see how many men and women and children were sleeping on the streets, some blocking off a road, lane, or alley at night and simply lying there on a sheet or piece of cardboard. Once it began to rain people would remain standing and wait for dawn while holding tiny, writhing, wet-to-the-bone children in the arms. These children, in many ways, are a symbol of the Haiti that is to come. We can either shield and protect them from a very difficult start or we can turn away and let their stories and voices fade, which would almost be the same as letting them die.

The young people of Youth Communication have decided not to let these voices fade or die. In doing this, they are honoring a generation of their peers who in less than a minute watched everything they have ever known crumble or vanish. Haiti is on the mind of these talented young writers at this moment just as it is on the minds of many others. However, even before this disaster, as these essays poignantly show, Haiti was already deep in the minds, and hearts, of the teen writers at Youth Communication.

I had the honor of writing for Youth Communication when I was in high school and have the even greater honor of having two of my own teenage essays included in this book. The writing and publication of these essays were milestones in my life. The essays, if nothing else, show how for some of us Haiti has never been a distant place. Now, by publishing this book, we hope to make this true for everyone else.

Haiti will constantly need our attention, our empathy—frankly our help—for at least the next 10 years. It does not need our pity though. More than anything else it needs our understanding. Our understanding of its complexity. Our understanding of its triumphs and failures. Our understanding of its humanity. This is what I hope that you, the reader of this wonderful and timely book, will get from the essays here.

"*Nou bite men nou pa p tonbe,*" declares one Haitian proverb. It means, "We have stumbled, but we will not fall." I have no doubt that Haiti will rebuild, not only because Haitian men and women are resourceful and resilient, but because they simply must. However, as Haiti's friends and neighbors and Haitians themselves look forward to what we all hope will be a stronger and better Haiti, we must also look back at the strong and glorious nation that Haiti has always been, a nation that has at times stumbled, but has never completely fallen. *Wi, nou bite, men nou pa p tonbe.*

Just as we have in the past, Haitians will turn this tragedy into an opportunity to remake our country and ourselves. I am sure of it. How can we not, with voices like the ones you are about to read standing with us? As the former ambassador to Haiti, the late, great African-American intellectual Frederick Douglass, once said, "Haiti will remain in the firmament of nations, and, like the star of the north, will shine on and shine on forever."

Reading the essays I have absolutely no doubt about that.

Edwidge Danticat
April 12, 2010

Introduction

By Dana K. Vincent

According to the latest U.S. Census report there are nearly 800,000 Haitian-Americans in the United States. Another 70,000 live in Canada. You may have heard of the acclaimed writer Edwidge Danticat, or the singer Wyclef Jean. If you live in a major Eastern city like Miami, New York, Boston, or Montreal, chances are you may know someone who is Haitian.

But a quick game of word association. Before January 12, 2010, what came to your mind when you heard the words "Haiti" or "Haitians"? Do these words and phrases ring a bell?

Boat people
Political instability
Illegal aliens
Refugees
Nothing like me at all
Poorest country in the Western Hemisphere

Since January 12, 2010, the word "earthquake" is probably what comes to mind when you hear the word "Haiti." Since that day, images of the incomprehensible devastation and an out-pouring of international support for the country and its children have left a lasting impression. You yourself may have donated to the relief efforts or know people who have been affected.

The first essay in this book, "Tomorrow Is Promised to No One," by Cassandra Charles, deals with the loss the earthquake visited on her family. But this book is about much more than the earthquake.

It is a compilation of essays written by Haitian-American teens who, like me, participated in the Youth Communication writing program over the course of the last 25 years. The essays address the Haitian immigrant experience and its intersection with broader teen experiences. Some of these essays explore issues that are specific to Haitians, like risking their lives to come to America in leaky boats. But most of the stories explore issues that are common to all teens, like the feeling of wanting to fit in, the process of learning to stand up for ourselves and what we believe, the struggle to overcome our fears and accept change, and the challenge of finding the beat of our own drum and the courage to dream our own dreams.

These stories invite teen readers to see themselves in the experiences of Haitian-American youth. And the more readers relate to the issues describe, the more likely they are to understand the importance of learning to say, as Marsha Dupiton does, "Yeah, I'm Haitian and I am proud." Whether we are from China or California, Pakistan or Pennsylvania, Belgium or Brooklyn, cultural and national pride—how we see ourselves and others see us—is important to all of us. This book tackles that universal theme, through the lens of the Haitian-American experience.

Cassandra Worrell's piece, "Haiti's Part in America's History" provides some historical background for Haitian pride. (Cassaundra is the only writer in this anthology who is not Haitian. But more than 20 years ago, when she was a teenager, Haiti was in the news every day as the country struggled to emerge from many years of brutal dictatorship. Writing the article was her way of trying to make sense of the news, and sharing what she learned with her peers. In its largest sense, that is the mission of this entire anthology.)

In "Finding My Haitian Pride," Marsha Dupiton writes that being Haitian was something she took so totally for granted that it was like "breathing air or drinking water." When she discovers that her friends have ignorant stereotypes about Haitians, she reacts at first by trying to play down her heritage. But over time, she realizes a desire to show others a more accurate view of Haitian culture.

Most of these writers recognize that they are safer and have greater opportunities in America, for which they are grateful. Yet when they come up against anti-Haitian prejudice, it threatens their sense of belonging here. Natalie Neptune was actually born on a boat traveling from Haiti to America. (When her father told her she was born on the ocean, she thought she was a mermaid.) By her late teens she is on track to becoming an American citizen. But when a Haitian immigrant is brutalized by the New York City police she questions whether racism and bigotry so compromise the American dream that she should reconsider ("What Happened to My American Dream?").

While essays like Natalie's address assimilation and other "big" ideas of the immigrant experience, the strength in these stories lies equally in the slices of everyday teen experience they offer. Maybe you can relate to the boy who falls in love, only to lose the girl when they both move away from their hometown (David Etienne in "Dream Girl"). Or maybe you can understand the impulse that moves Kaela Bazard to give away her dolls and teddy bears to her friends when she moves, so they'll have something to remember her by ("I Found a Way to Make My New Country Home").

Many people are picked on at school for being different: Daniel Jean-Baptiste finds solace in the language of math ("Solitary Confinement in the 1st Grade"), while Elie Elius turns tough but discovers that harshness doesn't really work for him ("I Showed My Enemies, and Hurt My Friends Too"). Other writers describe memories both happy and bittersweet: Raelle Charles recalls how her father taught her to dance ("Moving to the Music") and how she lost a pair of gold earrings with sentimental value ("My Mother's Gift"). And while most people have never been separated from their parents for as long as Edwidge Danticat lived away from hers, many teens can relate to the experience of feeling alienated from their families ("A New World Full of Strangers").

It is our hope that the next time you hear the words "Haiti" or "Haitians" you will remember these stories and think of yourselves.

1. JANUARY 12, 2010

TOMORROW IS PROMISED TO NO ONE

BY CASSANDRA CHARLES

January 15, 2010. It's 7 a.m. and the phone rings. My heart begins pounding. Since the earthquake hit Haiti three days earlier we haven't heard anything from our relatives, so each call poses a threat. I race to the phone and upon seeing the caller ID—it's my cousin in Haiti—I feel tears well up in my eyes. All I can think is, "She shouldn't be calling this early."

"Hello, Cassan, *eske mammi la? Mwen bezouin pale ak li.*" My cousin's voice sounds cold and broken as she asks, in Creole, to speak to my mother. I hand my mom the phone and without a

On January 12, 2010, Haiti suffered a devastating earthquake. More than 300,000 people died and a million were made homeless. The shockwaves were felt around the world, especially in Haitian communities. Cassandra Charles, living in New York City, describes the events and feelings she experienced in the first few days following the quake.

single word uttered between us, my mother's eyes and mine connect; a mutual transfer of fear and anguish is made.

A few seconds later, I hear my mom gasp and look down. My worst fears roar to life as she cries, "Baby *mouri*! Baby has died!" Rocks of saliva form and make it impossible for me to breathe or scream. I can't even move.

I don't know why, but I believed that my family would experience this tragedy with no real loss. When I heard my mother's words I found myself thinking: "This can't be true; my cousin is too young, too beautiful, too smart, too every good thing that exists; please, God, don't let it be true. She's only 20, her graduation is coming up, she has a beautiful nephew to meet, she has so much more living to do." I sat shaking my head, trying to make this whole thing a lie.

I met Alexandra, whom everyone called "Baby," for the first time when I traveled to Haiti eight years ago. I was 11 and she was 12. "*Allo, mwen se kouzin ou,*" she said, meaning, "Hello, I'm your cousin." We immediately hit it off and for the rest of my visit, we were inseparable.

We talked about how different life in America was and how life in Haiti was such an adventure every day. One day you could see a carnival right outside your window, and the next day a full brawl between street merchants. We teased her little brother who was always bothering us, and drank "*Kola Lakay,*" a Haitian drink that locals consider the official beverage of the nation, like nobody's business.

> **I BELIEVED MY FAMILY WOULD EXPERIENCE THIS TRAGEDY WITH NO REAL LOSS.**

"Baby" was such an open and caring person, a humble and beautiful soul. Her smile could light up an entire town, and it did: Everyone in her small town of Delmas 19 loved her and predicted she would go far in life.

When my mom hung up the phone, she explained that Baby had been at her college at the time of the earthquake. As my mom continued speaking, it was as if I became deaf; all I could picture was Baby under rubble, in pain, scared out of her mind. I felt every ounce of strength and hope drain from my body.

Then my mom jumped to her feet screaming, "Serge!! Serge!!" as it hit her that her brother had lost his daughter. "We have to go to him now! Get ready!"

My uncle and two of his children live here in New York, while his wife and the other children live in Haiti. Like my mom, I was suddenly hit by the realization that my other cousin

A SUDDEN DESPERATE URGE TO BE WITH THEM AROSE IN ME.

had lost her only sister, who was without a doubt her best friend. If I was in so much pain, I knew, she must be losing her mind. As it did in my mom, a sudden desperate urge to be with them arose in me, and I couldn't shower and dress quickly enough.

This is how the earthquake hit my family, and I found strength in comforting family members who were in more pain than I was. I'd heard it said that a person can be in so much pain that you feel it coming off their body, but experiencing it was like nothing I had ever felt. When I embraced my cousin at my uncle's house, her body felt so limp and hot that I was afraid she would get sick from crying so hard.

I felt myself close to losing it, but I knew that I had to be strong for her, for her little brother, and for my uncle. I walked away and gathered myself, and then I came back in and sat in silence holding her little brother's hand.

Now that it's been a few days, I can actually sit and write about what's happened, but getting to this point has been an uphill battle. It's hard to accept I'll never see my cousin again. I found myself asking God if he had to take someone from my family, why not an old person, someone who had lived their life?

This earthquake taught me that tomorrow is promised to no one, so we should all live our lives to the fullest and try to make sure they are worthwhile. It has reminded me to be kind to people and loving to family, friends, and even myself.

Cassandra was 19 when she wrote this story
and in her first year of college.

THINK ABOUT IT

Has a natural disaster—a hurricane, flood, earthquake, etc.—ever affected your family? If so, what impact did it have and how did your family deal with it?

Are you separated by long distance from a family member? How does that affect your relationship? (Or, have you ever felt you had to be strong for someone else, even though you were upset or scared yourself? What was that like? In the end, do you think that thinking of the other person's needs made your own experience harder, or more manageable?)

What does Cassandra mean when she writes that "tomorrow is promised to no one?"

II. Finding My Haitian Pride

I MAY NOT LOOK HAITIAN, BUT...

BY MARSHA DUPITON

I had just started junior high at a diverse school where the cliques were based on ethnicity and coolness. I didn't really belong to a clique, and considered myself a normal preteen who didn't care much about the social ladder. That is, until one day in homeroom when we started talking about where everyone came from.

"OK, class, now that we've finished our unit on different heritages, we're going to speak about your cultures and how they differ from each other," said my 6th grade homeroom teacher, Ms. Rose. I was excited. I loved hearing about other cultures. And I was eager to speak about my rich Haitian-American culture, especially the food. Picture a plate piled high with red beans so piping hot that you're afraid you'll burn your tongue, a fried beef dish called *taso*, and on the side, corn, baby carrots, string beans,

> *Marsha never really thinks about being Haitian, until one day in class when she is made painfully aware of some of her classmates' misconceptions.*

and broccoli all sautéed together.

Everyone started talking about their heritage—Trinidadian, Jamaican, African-American, Middle Eastern, Jewish, Italian, and Asian. Finally it was my turn. I was excited and nervous, hoping I didn't butcher the Creole words that I was about to sprinkle into my talk.

"I am Haitian-American—" I said. And that's about as far as I got.

The comments started coming fast and furious. "Whoa, you don't even look like you Haitian!" and, "Your hair isn't nappy like the other Haitians'!" I was speechless. Why were my classmates reacting this way? They acted like being Haitian was a disease or something.

To me, being Haitian was like breathing air or drinking water. It was the smell of cornmeal and fish in the morning at my grandmother's house, the sweet sound of Haitian *kompa* music. Being Haitian was something I had never really thought about, but I knew it made me who I was.

"Are you sure you're not mixed with something?" one classmate asked. In the end, I said I was, because no way did I want to be associated with the negative ideas my classmates seemed to have about Haitians. Junior high was a jungle and I wasn't going to become prey.

> **THEY ACTED LIKE BEING HAITIAN WAS A DISEASE OR SOMETHING.**

Most of my Haitian friends were born here like me, and though we grew up with Haitian culture, we are also American. When I first saw the immigrant kids in junior high, I felt a little jealous that they got the richness and the culture of Haiti firsthand. I'd only been to Haiti a few times myself. During one visit when I was 7, I went to a friend's farm where she picked me a mango off one of her many fruit trees. When I finished eating it all, my hands were sticky and my belly was satisfied. That's what Haiti did for me—filled me with its sweet culture and made me feel content.

But after the kids' comments in homeroom that day, I saw the Haitian kids through my classmates' eyes for the first time. Different-colored clothes, nappy hair, and the thickness of their accent on their tongues. They sat in a corner of the lunchroom, looking like they had just come off the boat. They were so foreign and new and…countrified. One girl particularly fit the stereotype. She wore worn-out Converse sneakers and a lime green shirt, and her hair was in huge twists and barrettes. She looked like a big 2-year-old.

They looked happy, speaking in their native tongue, Creole (or *Kreyòl*), which I understood and spoke. But I felt distant from them, even a bit superior. Although I didn't look stereotypically Haitian, after that day I started to change my appearance even more to secure a decent spot on the social ladder. It was survival of the coolest.

The first thing that had to change was my hair. My hair wasn't coarse—it was soft and curly and incredibly long, almost down to the middle of my back. But I still felt I needed to change it because straight was "in."

When I got home from the beauty salon, I stood in front of the mirror in my room. I took my head tie off and slowly unwrapped my hair, letting it cascade down my shoulders. It felt weird, as if the puffy cloud of hair that used to be there had been replaced with a silky, straight wig. When I stared at my reflection in the mirror, I felt pleased but empty, as if I'd eaten a piece of chocolate cake too fast. I didn't "look Haitian," that's for sure, but I didn't look like Marsha either.

Then I began to care more about my clothing. Everything in my closet was from the Gap, which was OK. But Rocawear and Baby Phat were considered the "best of the best," and something Haitians would never wear. So I began to wear a few articles of clothing from urban clothing stores like these and Lot 29.

I changed at home, too. When my parents and grandparents spoke to me in Creole or French, I would answer in English. They were frustrated with me, especially my grandmother. They felt that I was being arrogant with my refusal to speak anything but English.

With the "improvement" of the fresh Nike kicks on my feet and permed hair that framed my face, none of my peers suspected I was even partly Haitian anymore. When anyone asked me what I was, I would say that I was American, which was half truth and half lie.

For the rest of junior high, I was accepted. But in the end, my new image left me ashamed. I was covering up who I really was, the part of me that loved the Haitian music I listened to in my dad's car and the food that made my stomach so happy. But I continued to ignore my Haitian heritage because it felt more important to be accepted by my peers than for me to identify who I actually was.

After 8th grade, I started attending a high school where there seemed to be no Haitian immigrants to embarrass me. Then, the summer after freshman year, I stumbled upon a poem on my cousin's MySpace page.

The poem was called "I Don't Look Haitian?" by Prosper Sylvain Jr., a Haitian poet. It was about the stereotypes that people have about Haitians and how we are much smarter, stronger, and wiser than many people think. After I read it, I felt empowered, as if Sylvain's poem was an elixir that had revived and restored the balance of my two heritages.

The lines that inspired me the most were: "I don't look, sound, or act Haitian?/ Why?/ Is it because I do not have the seawater of Biscayne Bay/ dripping from my tattered clothes,/ or is it because I am not always dark as you perceived me to be,/ did I mess up your entire theory of relativity,/ that all relatives of Haitians must be dark and/ comely, like the tents of your media's Kedar?" ("The tents of Kedar" are mentioned in the Bible's Song of Solomon; the people who lived in them were considered dark-skinned outsiders.)

A few days later, after reading this part over and over again, I began to reevaluate my position in the Haitian-American community. Was I to sit back and let the views of ignorant people about Haitians persist? Prosper Sylvain put himself out there with his poem, refusing to let stereotypes define him. He showed that a Haitian is capable of creating powerful poems like Maya Angelou's. He defended and protected his heritage. I wanted to be like him, someone who wasn't afraid to say, "Yeah, I am Haitian and I am proud!"

> **I STARTED TO CHANGE MY APPEARANCE. IT WAS SURVIVAL OF THE COOLEST.**

What better way to prove myself than on Flag Day, a day when you can represent and embrace your culture to the fullest? Flag Day was first started to celebrate the American flag, but many people in Brooklyn, especially those who come from immigrant families like I do, use this day to show where their ancestors came from.

I came to school decked out in three Haitian flags: one around my waist and two on my wrists. The flags bled the colors red, white, and blue (ironically American colors, too) onto my body. On my head I wore a Haitian flag bandanna. I looked great and everyone complimented my outfit. I was beaming and extremely proud. It was my first step toward acknowledging who I was and defending my ancestral country.

That day, it was as if God was putting me to the test to see if I had truly embraced my heritage and was not bluffing. I was the only one at school who was wearing the Haitian flag. There were many other Haitian-American students, but many were mixed with something else and had chosen to represent the more "presentable" side of their ethnicity.

A Trinidadian girl came up to me and asked me where all the rest of my "people" were. I told her that I didn't know, but I was going to represent Haiti even if I didn't have anyone to celebrate with me.

She laughed and said, "Maybe they're hiding."

Had I heard right? Had she just blatantly disrespected my heritage? "Um, no one's hiding," I said. "Obviously you see that I am here. Just because I don't have a number of people with me representing Haiti doesn't mean anything." I felt like a rebel, speaking out to those who felt the need to stomp my culture to the ground. The girl walked away, having nothing more to say.

> I WAS THE ONLY ONE WEARING THE HAITIAN FLAG.

I know I'm not the only Haitian who went through this phase of hiding my heritage; many of my friends did the same thing in junior high school.

It's hard to embrace a heritage that gets bagged on by everyone. But it's also important to never forget who you are and where your ancestors came from.

Today, I hang with a rainbow of ethnicities. I try to learn about other people's cultures and make sure that they get the right representation of mine. I tell them about my childhood trips to Haiti and about the good stuff—Haiti's sandy beaches and blue-green water, its hospitality and generosity and the vibrancy of the country as a whole. I tell them Haiti was the first independent black republic in the world. I ask them to remove the stereotypical images from their minds, things like us eating sugar cane morning, noon and night, because it is hurting our real image as a people.

Now when I think about the first time I saw the Haitian kids in my school, I think about their smiles and how comfortable they seemed, switching between English and Creole. I realize now that because they were so comfortable in their own skins, it made me uncomfortable in mine. They didn't seem to see that people were talking about them, or they just didn't care.

Not embracing my heritage is impossible now, even if it's sometimes hard to balance it with my American upbringing. It's engraved in my mind and it's there to stay. As the poet Sylvain wrote, "My only nationality IS defined in three letters. I E T!" (Ay-ee-tee is how we pronounce "Haiti" in Creole.) Even though I am an American-born citizen, I know I will never disown the "Haitian" in me.

Marsha Dupiton graduated from high school and attended the State University of New York at Geneseo.

THINK ABOUT IT

Have you ever been misunderstood or teased because of your race or religion, or the neighborhood or country you came from? How did it affect the way you saw yourself? Did you stand up for yourself, or keep quiet and hope the teasing would just stop? What were the consequences? How do you feel about them now? Do you wish you had reacted differently? Why or why not?

Have you ever hidden or changed your identity to fit in with others? Did that help you or hurt you? Did you feel like you were betraying your "true" self, or just trying on another role?

Did you ever learn that something you thought was completely "normal" about yourself (such as your accent or the way you dress) was something that other people thought was "different?" What was it? Did it change your view of yourself in any way? How did their opinion make you feel?

III. Getting Started in America

MY MOTHER RISKED HER LIFE FOR US

BY GERTY JEAN-LOUIS

About eight years ago, when I was 8, I was living with my mom, dad, brother, and grandmother in Haiti when the country went into political turmoil. My father was in the military and he was assassinated a month after the turmoil began. We were left with nothing.

Because my father had been a captain in the military, we enjoyed political favor; once he was gone, that ended. My mother was left entirely on her own. She was inexperienced in life because she married at 16 and never worked outside our home.

Things were very bad for us. Hunger struck. That's when my mother decided to flee the country and settle in America to better

This is a winning essay from a 1994 contest in which teens were asked to write about a woman they admire. Gerty Jean-Louis picks her mother because of her courage and persistence.

our lives. But in America she would have no friends and no family. Nevertheless, she decided to leave Haiti. We were left behind with our grandmother.

Setting sail at night as one of many passengers on a broken down vessel, my mother spent two and a half months at sea with no land in sight. The food supply ran out five weeks after the journey began and she thought that she was going to die. The only things she had were our pictures, faith in God, and hope. Those three things kept her going as she lay weak from starvation. Two corpses were thrown overboard during the journey and she believed she was going to be the third.

> **MY MOTHER SPENT TWO AND A HALF MONTHS AT SEA.**

When she finally arrived in America, my mother was put into a detention camp for refugees. That place was like hell. There was little food. Since she was the new kid in the cell, she was beaten and picked on. She cried herself to sleep for many nights. After many long prayers she was let out.

My mother joined a refugee program where she was sheltered and clothed. She got a job working in a factory and slaved until she saved enough money to send for my little brother and me a year and a half later.

When I think about the things my mother has been through my admiration deepens, and all I can do is cry and cry. It's hard to believe that she risked her life to come to a new and strange land where she knew no one, all for her children.

A few months after our arrival, my mom enrolled in school. She got a GED, attended a nursing program, and is now a nurse's aide. She has become successful as the breadwinner in our family.

My mother, Evelyne, is the only one I look up to. I have just one goal and that's to one day say, "Mom, you've done more than enough. It's time to relax. Let me take care of you now. Let me pay you back for your priceless love. You deserve it, and so much more. I just hope that one day I can be as great a mother as you are."

Gerty Jean-Louis was in high school when she wrote this story for the Barnard College "Woman I Admire" writing contest.

THINK ABOUT IT

Gerty's mom risks her life for her children. What do you think about her choice? Who in your life has made sacrifices to help you? How do you feel about their sacrifices? Did they take too big a risk? Could they have done more? Explain.

What family member do you admire the most, and why?

A NEW WORLD FULL OF STRANGERS

BY EDWIDGE DANTICAT

I could hear nothing over the deafening engine of the airplane, but I certainly could see their faces. They waved wildly as though this was a happy occasion. They seemed so thrilled that I was finally going off to the rich and prosperous city of New York. I was sad beyond the limits of my 12 years of life.

One of the stewardesses grabbed me from the doorway and quickly led me inside. Their waves. . . their smiles. . . their cheers were no more. I solemnly followed her to the seat I was to take. She flashed her smile and I was left alone for the trip.

The tears that I'd fought so bravely before fell uncontrollably

Edwidge did not have to brave a rickety boat come to America like Gerty's mother in the previous story. Instead, she flew safely on a plane. But it was still traumatic to leave the country and people she loved, to reunite with her family after 10 years apart, and to adjust to "a new world full of strangers."

into my lap. I was leaving my aunt, uncle, and countless cousins to embark on a mysterious trip to be with parents I barely knew and brothers I'd never met.

The stewardess woke me when the plane landed. Before I knew what was happening, she and I were filing down an endless tunnel toward what seemed like a crowd of caretakers.

First the people who made alien cards pulled me aside and snapped my picture. Then the people who handled the bags rushed me through a line to grab my suitcase. Soon, ahead of the other passengers, I was walking through the gates to the meeting area of the terminal.

I DID NOT REMEMBER WHAT MY PARENTS LOOKED LIKE.

Since I did not remember what my parents looked like, I was very frightened when a tall bearded man started to hug me. I was even more afraid when a chubby woman placed her arms around me and exclaimed, "At last my little girl is home!" I felt like an orphan who was being adopted against her will.

The ride home was no more comforting than the meeting with my parents. I was uncomfortably squashed between my three brothers in the back seat of the car while my parents and uncle were crowded in the front seat.

My American brothers, who had given me timid hugs before piling into the car, were now curiously staring at me. I imagined they were as anxious to know where I'd come from as I was to know where I was going.

Perhaps if they had asked me who I was, I would have explained that it was not my fault at all that I was entering their lives after so many years apart.

To feed and clothe our family, my parents had to desert me so early in life that now I did not even know them. The boys had probably heard about the problems in Haiti: the poverty, the oppression, the despair. I wanted to plead with them to accept me, not stare at me. But I suddenly realized that they had every right to stare. I was, after all, a stranger—even to my own family.

To avoid their glares, I turned to the car window. There must have been hundreds of thousands of lights speeding by. I tried to imagine how many millions of dollars it must have taken to bathe the city in such brightness. God, I thought, this must be the richest country on the planet.

Our home was a great disappointment. It was a two-bedroom apartment on the sixth floor of a graffiti-covered building. In Haiti, homes were almost always open and spotless. In my new building, the doors were shut and dusty.

I COULD NOT UNDERSTAND WHAT WAS BEING SAID AROUND ME.

When we reached the apartment my parents lived in, I hesitated before going inside. The door looked like a cage. When my father fastened the filthy lock, I felt like I was in prison.

My parents did not wait long to enroll me in school. I could barely tell the difference between "hi" and "high" before I found myself in the car heading for IS 320. The school building had even more graffiti than the apartment building.

In Haiti, schools and churches were treated with utmost respect. Here things were obviously not the same. I wanted to run back to the car as my father and I walked by a crowd of hysterical students. In my pink cotton dress and yellow sneakers, I was sure they were laughing at me.

As we entered the building, I held my father's hand so tightly one would have thought that my life depended on it. In my school back home, I had been the best memorizer and the most articulate student. I had never given any teacher reason to hit me. Here I was sure that I would fail no matter how hard I tried.

Fortunately, there was a Haitian gentleman in the office. He had a brief talk with my father and made him sign some papers.

Then the gentleman walked me to my homeroom class. As I left my father to go fight my way past the shoves of the hurried students in the halls, I felt as though I had been abandoned once again.

The Haitian gentleman introduced me to the homeroom teacher and then to one of the many Haitian girls in the class. He told me that she was one of the most respected girls in the school, mostly because of her roughness. The first day, my new friend kindly escorted me from class to class and made me sit next to her in every one.

Despite her help, I could not understand what was being said around me. As far as I was concerned, the teachers might as well have been hitting spoons against the blackboards. I understood nothing. The classes all blended into one long, discouraging day. To make things worse, each time I stepped into the halls the thought of being abused by the other students scared me.

My fear was not realized until the last period, when our class ate lunch. One of the girls on the lunch line lifted my skirt up in the air and began to laugh. During her fit of laughter, she managed to spit out the word "Haitian" as though it were the filthiest and funniest word she'd ever said in her entire life.

Because my friend intervened, my humiliation that day was brief. After everyone found out that I was always with her, no one tried to touch me again.

Unfortunately, the verbal abuse did not stop. "Haitians are filthy. They have AIDS. They stink." Even when I could not understand the actual words, the hatred with which they were expressed hurt me deeply.

Now that I've grown to understand every insult, they hurt even more. In the same way that my brothers glared at me my first day in this country, people often glare at me as though searching for some sign of my nationality. If I don't fit their particular stereotype, they challenge me. They ask me whether I am sure that I am really Haitian.

Being any kind of immigrant isn't easy. Nevertheless, the view of Haitian immigrants has made us ashamed among our peers. The boat people and those few stricken with AIDS have served as profiles for all of us.

If only those who abuse us would ask, perhaps we'd explain that it is not our fault that we are intruding on their existence. To avoid brutal deaths and lead better lives, we are forced to leave our homes.

We'd plead with them to accept us and accommodate us, not make life miserable for us. Because, yes, we are strangers. Unfortunate strangers in a world full of strangers.

Edwidge graduated from high school and college and became a writer. Her writing exploring Haitian and Haitian-American themes—including, Brother I'm Dying *(see pp. 136 for a review), and* Breath Eyes Memory*—have won wide acclaim, including a MacArthur Fellowship.*

THINK ABOUT IT

Have you ever felt like a stranger to your own family? Why did you feel that way? How did you handle it?

Have you ever had to adjust to a new school or neighborhood? What was hardest about it?

SOLITARY CONFINEMENT IN THE 1ST GRADE

BY DANIEL JEAN-BAPTISTE

At about the age of 6, I found out that I was going to be traveling to the United States from Haiti. I didn't really expect the move to change anything. I thought that maybe I would have a few more toys and a bigger television, but I never imagined my life would be so completely different.

I found out otherwise on my first day of school. It was about a month into the school year when I walked into the 1st grade class with my parents. It was a brightly decorated room filled with letter combinations, which meant nothing to me. I was the center of attention and was being studied by everyone in the room.

Suddenly, I was nervous. I could only speak Creole, even

Daniel struggles mightily as a new immigrant who does not speak English. But when he realizes that numbers are a universal language and discovers his own resilience, he begins to find a path in America.

though my parents had been trying to cram some of the English words and phrases they considered vital into my head. One phrase they continually emphasized was, "Teacher, this boy is bothering me." Obviously my parents knew something I didn't.

First I had to say my name. Everyone said, "Huh?" I said my name again. They said "Huh?" again. The vicious cycle continued until the teacher broke it by saying my name one syllable at a time.

I WAS THE ONLY ONE IN THE CLASS WHO COULDN'T SPEAK ENGLISH.

After my parents left I felt even worse. I couldn't communicate with anyone, including the teacher. She did nothing to try to make me feel like part of the class and there was nothing that she could do. I spent the whole day looking around the room at all the things I couldn't understand. Sometimes I would stare out the window at the playground. Whenever I tried to pay attention I became upset because I had no idea what anyone was saying.

"Where are all the bilingual teachers my parents told me would be here to help me?" I wondered. "How am I supposed to learn this dumb language if there's no one to teach me?" As far as I knew, I was the only one in the class who couldn't speak English. I felt different from everyone else and didn't like the feeling.

The other students looked at me like it was my fault I couldn't speak their language. It was like they were saying, "What do you mean you can't speak English? All the rest of us can speak English. I can, he can, she can; why can't you?"

I would have sworn it was impossible to feel more isolated and rejected than I did in that classroom, but I would have been wrong. Recess was a double portion of loneliness. It was like being in prison at the tender age of 6 and having to watch other children play through the bars on your cell. The joy, fun, and laughter were there. I just couldn't be a part of it. I guess it wasn't their fault. After all, how could they have explained a game of tag to me? What bothers me is the fact that they didn't even try.

There's one day in particular that I will never forget. It was another lonesome day at the playground and, by then, everyone knew I was the new kid who spoke no English and had no friends. I was walking around, as I usually did, watching the others play and asking myself, how come there are so many children and I'm so lonely?

Somewhere between my steps and my thoughts two kids walked up to me and asked me the strangest questions. Of course, I didn't understand what they were saying. After the inquisition, one of them grabbed me from behind while the other tried to beat me up. Even though I couldn't understand their words, I was able to perceive their hatred.

All of this completely scrambled my emotions and my thoughts. At first I had been determined to learn the language so that I could participate, but after the playground incident, my determination was almost completely obliterated. I felt angry and discouraged. "Why even bother?" I asked myself.

This went on for weeks until finally—miracle of miracles!— the teacher entered linguistically neutral territory. I was looking out the window when the kid next to me, Joseph, passed me a sheet of paper. Great,

> **TWO WAS TWO IN ANY LANGUAGE.**

I thought to myself, more things for me not to understand. Well, guess what? I saw NUMBERS. WOW! It was math. I was ecstatic, because finally something I learned back in Haiti was of some use to me. I didn't have to be able to speak English to do math. Two was two in any language. Two plus two was still four.

My loneliness came to an end, temporarily, when a couple of my classmates found out that I was good at math. They wanted my answers, but since we couldn't communicate, I couldn't share them. I would have if I could because the emotional quarantine had become so unbearable. I wanted to belong so much that I was willing to do something I never would have considered in my country—cheat.

Eventually, I learned to speak English. Things changed for me after that, but not completely. I find that people have stereotypes about Haitian immigrants that affect us whether we speak English or not. These stereotypes were set in the minds of these people way before I arrived at the airport, and most of them are negative. I was able to break away from the stereotypes by showing, through what I do and say, that they don't apply to me—that I am intelligent, that I can learn a new language, and that I am not afraid of the people who disrespect me.

Daniel graduated from high school and later got a degree in computer science from Columbia University.

THINK ABOUT IT

Have you ever been in a situation where most people spoke a language you didn't understand? What was the experience like?

Have you ever felt separated from your classmates because of a big difference between you? Were you able to overcome those differences and become friends? How?

Imagine you were placed in an entirely new setting where you didn't know the people or the language. Is there a "universal" language you could use to make connections—such as numbers, music, or dance? How would using this "universal" language help bridge the gap between you and the new people you meet?

I FOUND A WAY TO MAKE MY NEW COUNTRY HOME

BY KAELA BAZARD

"We're moving to America, honey!" my mother announced as we sipped our coffee on a hot Saturday morning during the summer before 5th grade.

I stared at her, hoping she would say "psych!" or make some gesture to tell me she was joking. But to my surprise, she kept the confident face she wore only when she was really determined.

My grandmother had emigrated to the U.S. before I was born. My mother was always telling me that my grandmother had applied for our permanent residency and we'd move there when all the papers were sorted out. But I never took her seriously because she'd been saying that since I was 4. So I was shocked when she popped the news that we were moving, along with my

At first, Kaela does not want to move from Haiti to the United State, and she has a hard time adjusting to the new country. But eventually she loses her fear of change.

HAITI ON MY MIND

stepfather and uncle.

"But I don't want to move. What about my friends? Can't we move next year?" I asked.

"I understand, but we'll have a better life in America," she replied. "You'll have a better education, and you can always make new friends."

"I could always stay with one of my aunts and visit you during the summer. Please, I'm begging you to let me stay!" I pleaded with her.

BEING SO FAR AWAY IN ANOTHER COUNTRY TERRIFIED ME.

"I'm not about to go halfway around the world and leave you!" she snapped. "You're moving. End of story!"

I had always thought of myself as open and independent. I had my first sleepover when I was 4. I often visited the countryside with my church or school for at least a month at a time. I can't remember one time in my life when I felt homesick.

I guess that was because I knew that sooner or later the vacation would be over and I'd return home. But this time I was leaving for good. The thought of being so far away in another country terrified me.

I lived in an apartment with my mother, stepfather, and uncle in Port-au-Prince, the capital of Haiti. We had a comfortable life there. I couldn't understand why my mother wanted to move. I went to private school and she had a stable job as a salesperson. But deep down, I knew she had a point. Things weren't that great for her financially and if we moved to the U.S., she wouldn't have to spend so much money on my education.

Plus, she was pregnant. She wanted the best for my soon-to-be-born brother, and private school in Haiti was very expensive. So to my mom, it seemed like a perfect time for a new start. The only problem was that I didn't want a new start. For several nights, we had endless arguments during which I tried convince her to let me stay with my aunt for a year until I graduated from elementary school.

One night, my mom got tired of my nagging and proposed a compromise. I would live in the U.S. with her for a year. If I still felt the same way at the end of the year, she'd gladly send me back to Haiti to live with my relatives.

My mom was very clever about it. She knew that by the end of a whole year, I'd forget about my life in Haiti and adopt my new life in America. I rejected the idea instantly and told her that I knew what she was up to.

My mother got angry and told me that since I refused to even try, I'd have to move right away, with no compromises. That was the last time we argued about it. I'd have to watch myself helplessly slip off the Haitian island and there was nothing I could do.

I spent my last two weeks visiting all my favorite hangouts. I ate a lot of sugarcane, mangos, and many other juicy fruits so my mouth wouldn't forget their unique tropical tastes. It was an unbearable heartbreak for me to say goodbye to my two best friends, Daphne and Stephanie. We'd been friends since we were in diapers. Knowing we wouldn't be in each other's daily lives anymore felt devastating.

I'D FORGOTTEN TO ASK MY COUSIN HOW TO PRONOUNCE MY NAME IN ENGLISH.

On the day of our flight, my mom, uncle, and I sat in the airport (my stepfather was planning to join us later). All I had with me were some clothes. I'd given everything else, including my dolls and my teddy bear collection, to my friends so they would remember me. I felt like a wild fish that had been taken away from the sea to be put into an aquarium full of fish different from itself.

Two weeks later, I found myself in 5th grade in Brooklyn. It was the first day of school. "What's your name?" a short black lady asked me.

I just stared at her. I'd grown up speaking French and Haitian Creole, and I didn't understand anything that came out of her mouth.

For days I'd been standing in front of the mirror, practicing the English words that my Brooklyn cousin had helped me memorize. I'd learned the ABC's and basic sentences like "I need to use the bathroom" and "What time is it?" But as I stared at the teacher, I felt so shy that they all vanished from my mind.

> **I GOT TIRED OF BEING MISERABLE AND FEELING SORRY FOR MYSELF.**

"What's your name, dear?" she asked again. I finally figured out what she was asking. The problem was that throughout all the memorization and English practice, I'd forgotten to ask my cousin how to pronounce my name in English. What if it sounded funny in my native language and the other kids laughed at me?

"Ka-ye-la" my mouth answered, unaware of my nervous thoughts. I'd pronounced it in Creole. "Great!" I thought. "My first day and I screw up on my name. Way to go."

The teacher nodded and said, "Oh! Ke-o-la. Nice name."

Afraid of correcting her, I simply nodded back. Maybe that was the way it was pronounced in English. But it sounded like a barking dog in my ears.

The first month was difficult. I didn't have many friends like my mother had promised. Who would want to be around a person who didn't understand what you were saying? Some days I'd stay up past midnight with my bilingual dictionary, trying to understand an assignment. A month later, my English had improved a lot. But little did I know, my progress would end up backfiring and making me feel even more like an outsider.

It was right after lunch and the bell was ringing for the next class to start. As I hurried from the schoolyard to the fifth floor so I wouldn't be late, a security guard stopped me and looked at me furiously. "Young lady, why are you running in the hallways?" she asked.

"I-am-late for class," I answered in my awkward English.

"No. You're cutting class," she snapped.

I had no idea what "cutting" meant. But her facial expression looked so nasty that I knew she was accusing me of something.

"What?" I asked, looking confused and hoping she might repeat herself.

Instead she said, "Listen, you want to play games with me? I'll take you to the principal's office and we'll have a heck of a time."

"I don't understand what you're saying. I don't speak English!" I answered her in a panic, trying not to cry.

"What seems to be the problem?" I heard a lady ask from behind. When we both turned, I saw that it was my teacher. I'd never been so glad to see her.

"This student was pretending to be running late to class, and when I confronted her, she lied, saying that she doesn't speak English," the security guard said. "Her English sounds fine to me."

My teacher assured her that I was telling the truth. The security guard apologized and claimed that she could have sworn I spoke English perfectly.

Most people in my position would have been flattered. But I felt humiliated and misunderstood. If my teacher hadn't come out, I would have gotten in trouble for no reason. For days, I blamed myself for not knowing what to say.

My mother felt sorry for me and encouraged me to be more patient, reminding me that many kids come here from different countries and eventually learn the language. Every time she said this, my heart wanted to scream that I wouldn't be having to go through all this if it weren't for her. I'd been safe and comfortable in Haiti, instead of living in a cold, strange country that I'd never wanted to move to.

But after a few months I got tired of being miserable and feeling sorry for myself all the time. I wanted to be happy again more than anything. But for me, that meant mastering English, and I didn't think that I was smart or capable enough to do it.

I was in school one afternoon when I finally decided to fight for my happiness. The teacher had just called on me to read during a reading circle for the first time. My heart was beating so fast that it was hard to breathe. I started slowly, stumbling on some of the verbs, but I kept going until I'd read the whole page. When I finished, I was afraid to look up to see the expressions on my classmates' faces. When I finally did, I saw everyone, including the teacher, staring in amazement.

IT WAS UP TO ME TO MAKE IT A POSITIVE OR NEGATIVE EXPERIENCE.

"Wow, Ms. Jenkins, she can read," one girl exclaimed. They all started clapping. Right at that moment, I knew that my miserable days were over. My English wasn't perfect yet, but now I knew that I could master it, and I became determined to do whatever it took.

After that, I became determined to make the best of my new life in other ways, too. I slowly began to find things that I enjoyed about American culture. I hated the freezing weather during winter, but I loved how the streets were decorated with Christmas lights and angels.

I liked the tall skyscrapers in Manhattan and how brightly lit the streets were at night. I fell in love with window shopping at the mall, too. In Haiti, the stores weren't that close together or that big, and if you stared at some merchant's goods without buying anything, they'd curse at you in the blink of an eye.

Things were turning out well for my mother, too. After giving birth to my little brother, she'd gotten a job and was adjusting to American life as well.

A year later as we sat in the living room one evening, my mother asked me, "Do you still want to go back to Haiti?"

"Do you want to send me back?" I asked, laughing.

"Why not? My credit card would get a break," she joked in Creole.

"Well, I'm not going anywhere, Mom," I answered.

As she left the room, my mom said, "Aren't you the same girl who begged me to let her stay in Haiti?"

I thought about the question for a while and was confused. My old life seemed like a childhood memory. I still felt homesick sometimes and wanted to visit my friends and relatives, but my life was in New York.

I've been living here for seven years now. My memories of Haiti are still strong and I'm excited to go back to visit for the first time this summer. But I don't see myself living there permanently anymore, at least not anytime soon.

I guess I can thank my mother for forcing me out of my comfort zone and bringing me to a whole new world. I didn't choose to leave. But as I faced a new page in my life, it was up to me to make it a positive or negative experience. I'm glad I chose to make it positive.

Now I'm no longer fearful of whatever big changes life throws at me. I want to go away to college and travel to countries like France and Italy one day. My experience has shown me that no matter how scary it is to leave a place that's home, in time the new place will probably become twice as comfortable as the old one anyway.

Kaela graduated from high school and attended college.

THINK ABOUT IT

Have you ever had to make a big change in your life that you didn't want to make? Looking back, what was hardest about that change? How did it benefit you?

Kaela writes that she is no longer fearful of change; in fact, she thinks change is likely to bring better things. Do you agree? Why or why not?

Kaela is wrongly accused of cutting classes. Have you ever wrongly been accused of something? How did it make you feel?

IV. A GOAT, A GIRL, AND GOLDEN MEMORIES
Some Things We Left Behind

A GOAT NAMED MANUSH

BY DAVID ETIENNE

In Haiti, where I was born, the countryside is known as "the lost country" because people from the city don't know anything about it. City people sometimes make fun of country people and their accent, but I think country people are smarter than city people. City people depend on food transported from other countries, but country people are self-sufficient and grow and raise their own.

This isn't always easy, as I learned a few years ago. I lived in a rural town called Diegue. When I turned 7, my godmother gave me a baby goat. I had never dreamed of getting a goat for my birthday, but I was so happy. The goat was brown with a little bit of white on her face.

David grows up in the countryside, where he raises a pet goat that he grows very fond of—so fond that when it comes time to kill it for food he cannot bear the thought. When he moves to America, he still worries about the fate of his pet.

At first I left the goat untied because I wanted her to follow me around, until one day a man who lived nearby came to my house with a machete. He explained that the goat had eaten his crops, and if he found her in his garden ever again he would cut off her head. I decided it would be a good idea to tie my goat.

This goat and I became great friends. I even ate my dinner near her and fed her some of my rice. My older cousin Fabian also loved taking care of the goat and gave her the name "Manush." I liked it, so the goat now had a name. I promised my cousin that one day I would give her a baby goat like my godmother gave me.

> **BEFORE HE EVEN PUT THE KNIFE ON THE GOAT, I STARTED CRYING.**

After some time, we took Manush to a place where they had male goats and paid the owner to leave her there for one day. After a few months, she had three babies. I really wanted to give my cousin one, but I couldn't bear to give up any of them, so I asked her to wait until Manush had other babies.

After two years I had about seven goats and all of them were friendly. But I had a special relationship with Manush—some people say that dogs are man's best friend, but this female goat was mine.

When I turned 10 years old, my mother asked me if I wanted to eat one of the goats for my birthday. At that time nothing was in my mind except that I was about to eat a lot of meat, which I loved so much. Goat meat is one of the most expensive meats in Haiti, and I felt honored to have a whole goat cooked just for my birthday.

When my godfather was about to kill the goat (not Manush), he called me so I could hold its feet while he cut its throat. I was excited—some other kids were watching and this made me feel more grown-up and important than them.

I held the goat's legs, but before my godfather could even put the knife on the goat, I started crying. My hands were shaking. I suddenly felt as if the life of one of my best friends was about to be taken away. I felt weak and guilty knowing that I was going to play a part in killing my goat.

My brother called me soft and made me go away for the rest of the day. I went into the woods where I had put Manush and the rest of the goats. As soon as Manush saw me she started trying to come near me. I walked to her and petted her for a while.

I was thinking about the goat's head being cut off its body. To me it felt like a crime. Eventually my sister came to get me. I went home and sat at the table alone. Everyone was watching me as I ate the food, including the meat, with anger and sadness.

I tried hard not to let the goat's death affect me because I knew if I didn't get over it, my family and friends would make fun of me. On my next birthday they wanted to kill Manush, but I wouldn't let them, so they killed another of Manush's babies. Even though the goats belonged to me, I had no choice about this because everyone was waiting on the goat meat and the great-tasting soup my mother would make from it.

MY COUSIN TELLS ME MANUSH IS STILL ALIVE, BUT I DON'T BELIEVE HER.

Now that I live in America, it's nice not to have to eat one of my lovely goats every March 19th (my birthday), but the day still reminds me of them. It sounds thoughtful that my family would kill a goat just to please me, but my birthday has become one of the worst days of the year because I can't help thinking about the times when I had to eat creatures I cared about.

left Haiti on May 16, 2003, when I was 12. Two nights before I left, I went into the yard where the goats were and sat there talking to Manush. I knew I wasn't going to have any time to say goodbye if I didn't do it then. I felt like crying, but I didn't. I sat there petting Manush on the head, telling her that Fabian was going to take good care of her.

Now I live in a big city where I can find almost everything that I need, except for the atmosphere of the countryside—the aroma of coffee and fresh-made bread, roosters singing in the morning, the woods. I miss my favorite friend, Manush, most of all.

Two years ago I went to Haiti for a few days. When I asked about Manush my mother told me my godmother was watching over her, but when I asked to go see her, they never took me. That made me suspicious. Now my cousin tells me on the phone that Manush is still alive, but I don't believe her. It makes more sense that my family would sell her, because goats are worth a lot of money in Haiti.

Soon I will be going back there for another visit and will have the chance to see for myself, but I have a bad feeling. Everyone else thought of her as just a goat, but Manush was family to me.

David Etienne graduated from high school and enrolled in college. He also got involved in filmmaking as an actor and scriptwriter.

THINK ABOUT IT

David's family doesn't understand his love for his goat. Is there something your family doesn't understand about you? How does that affect your relationship with each other?

Manush is like family to David. Is there a pet—or a person who is not part of your blood family—who is like family to you? What do they provide that is important to you?

DREAM GIRL

BY DAVID ETIENNE

As a young boy in Haiti, I fell in love with every pretty girl who crossed before my eyes. Sometimes I would watch a movie and whatever the actor did to get the girl to kiss him, I would try too. I once made a Superman cape out of a piece of a sheet, put it on, and went up high in a mango tree to jump down, while a girl I liked was watching with a few of my friends.

I was so into impressing her that I forgot I was terrified of heights. Before I could jump I was already down. I fell off the branch and rolled down a little hill. Everyone laughed. After all this, the girl ended up moving the very next week. I felt so stupid.

In Haiti, our ambitions were based on what we saw on TV,

> *As a child, David had a severe crush on Mishland, a girl at his elementary school. He never saw her after she moved to another part of Haiti and he emigrated to the U.S. As a teenager, he realizes that Mishland represents a simpler life he has left behind forever.*

where everything looked better than what we were used to. Since a fancy life was out of reach for most of us, my friends and I would sometimes re-create scenes from movies we'd seen. Because of TV, we wanted to be rich and famous, heroic and strong. And even though we were little kids, we also wanted girlfriends.

But I didn't know how to approach girls. When I was 7 there was one pretty girl I especially adored, but I never took a chance on talking to her. She was my height and never braided her long, straight black hair. She was a member of her church choir and had the most beautiful voice. Her name was Mishland.

I never spoke to her until one day at lunchtime. The girls' bathroom had a problem, so the principal had students stand in a line to use the boys' bathroom. When I got to the front of the line, Mishland came out of nowhere and stood right in front of me.

"Can I please go in, I really have to use the restroom," she told me, squeezing her legs together.

Usually I would have said no, but I smiled and nodded. I had never expected her to even say hi to me, and at that moment I knew I had already fallen in love with her.

> **I WAS SO NERVOUS I COULDN'T EVEN STAND STRAIGHT.**

My best friend Herode wrote a love letter for me to give to her. I gave her the letter without reading it. The next day I received a letter from her with a lot of romantic pictures on it. It had only six words written in it, but I read it as if there were millions of words. It said in big letters, *Oui, j'aimerais être votre petite amie* ("Yes, I would love to be your girlfriend"). I took it home and hid it under my brother's mattress.

The next day the first person I saw at school was Mishland, waiting for me outside the schoolyard. I started shaking. I was so nervous I couldn't even stand straight. I didn't know how to be girlfriend and boyfriend, and I didn't think she knew much either. I wanted to tell her that she looked beautiful and smelled great, but I didn't even say "Hi." We both stood with our heads down, and I started kicking little rocks on the ground.

Out of nowhere came Herode. "'Sup, Etienne. Hey, Mishland," he said.

We both answered at the same time with a relieved, "Herode." He whispered to ask if I'd already kissed her.

"Relax, my friend, we have a lot of time to do that," I answered.

"Yeah," Mishland added.

"I bet you guys don't know how," Herode said.

I looked at him and looked at her. I thought about kissing her, and I thought about not doing it right. Almost against my will, I quickly kissed her on the lips and looked away. I wanted to look cool, so I didn't smile. I just walked away with Herode. I couldn't tell how Mishland reacted because I never looked back. All that was in my mind was that I was officially a cool person.

After that I was really happy to go to school. Before, the only time I would get a kiss was when I put my lips on my arm and pretended I was kissing a girl in a movie, but now I had a girlfriend and I could kiss her anytime I wanted. At first it was kind of weird kissing her, but soon we got more comfortable with each other and we loved nothing more than being with each other.

I liked Mishland because she was beautiful, and also smart and outgoing, the kind of person who respected everyone. And she brought out the best in me. When I started going out with her, I changed and acted more mature than I was.

Once, on a Saturday, I went to my father's farm and picked mangoes and avocadoes for her. I bought some bread and waited for her under a big tree near her house. When she arrived she thanked me with a kiss, and we sat there eating and talking about Haitian music. To me we looked like any other couple that loved each other.

Mishland and I were together for about five years, and we had all kinds of plans for our future life. We would get married, have two kids, and own a big house where our kids could run around all day and not get in our way.

I once had a dream where Mishland and I were cuddling on a white couch while our two kids ran around, and all of us were wearing white clothes. We were watching a Haitian movie about love. While the kids were playing, I gave Mishland a kiss on the forehead.

I've kept the memory of this little dream safe, deep down in my heart, for some time now. As time passes it gets shorter, and sometimes I have to make up things to give sense to it, because I keep forgetting parts of the sweetest dream I ever had.

One day when I was about 12, I found Mishland crying after school. When I asked what was wrong, she said she was going to move to another town and change schools. I forced myself to not cry. I hugged her and I could tell that she wanted me to say something nice to her, like "I won't ever forget about you." But nothing came to mind, so I said I would walk her home.

"Are you ever coming back?" I asked on the way.

"I don't know," she answered. "I'm going to live with my mother."

"Your mother is nice," I said. "If you ask her to bring you back here one day, would she do it?" She said she didn't know.

When we got to her house we stood in front of her door staring at each other, and then we started kissing. After a few minutes she went in and I sadly walked home.

The next day in school, she wasn't there. I tried so hard to not show others how sad I was, but I couldn't hide it. Tears were coming down my face. Where I lived it was rare for anyone to have a phone, so keeping in touch with someone who moved away was not so easy.

For a month of school, I barely laughed. I didn't play any

sports or participate in any dance competitions like I usually did. I thought about her night and day, hoping she would come back.

A few months later I found out that I was moving to the U.S. Unlike my brother, cousin, and sisters, I wasn't excited to come here. I was still crazy for Mishland and didn't see how America was going to help me fill the empty space that she had left.

Still, I tried to use the move to take my mind off her. I played football, basketball, soccer, and baseball in New York. I took up writing and acting, took care of my niece and nephew, and went out with other girls. I visited libraries all the time to read comic books. I tried every new thing that I thought would make me forget about her.

But I didn't forget. For the first three years that I lived in the U.S. I wrote many love stories with happy endings, based on the way I wished my relationship with Mishland had been. I wrote poems that were like a sheet to cover the missing part of my heart. None of the other girls I dated made me feel the same way she did, and I never took any of them as seriously as I took Mishland.

In some ways, trying to get over Mishland in the U.S. was better than if I had stayed in Haiti. Here, people didn't tease me about being in love at such a young age and I didn't have to stay away from places that would remind me of her. As time passed I met new people who loved me and took my mind off her. Eventually, with a new life and new things to think about, I began to let go of my sorrow over her.

AT FIRST IT WAS KIND OF WEIRD KISSING HER.

I don't know for sure what it would be like to see her again, and maybe it wouldn't be the same between us. But I'm curious about what it would be like, and sometimes it makes me sad that I don't know how she is doing and she doesn't know where I'm living. By now she's probably moved several times. Because life in Haiti is so hard, the best way to have a good life is to move wherever you can find a job.

Once, my whole idea of the world beyond Haiti was based on what I saw on TV. My dream was to grow up and marry Mishland, have children, and make enough money to afford a big house like I saw people had in America. Now that I live in the U.S., I still want the same things. Here I have a real opportunity to be successful, so I plan on making it happen. The only difference is that in my future family, my wife's picture is no longer Mishland, but a question mark.

When I used to watch love stories on TV, I had no idea what the true meaning of love was. I never expected to find someone in real life who loved me and that I would love back. But I did, and now I know what love is. Even though I don't expect Mishland and I will be together again, I still feel like we have a connection. It's like we're on the same page, but in different books.

It makes me miss the years we spent together, but I also feel alive when I think back on them. I've learned the only person who will be with me all through my life is myself, but I still appreciate Mishland as my first girlfriend, my first kiss, and my first dream that came true.

David Etienne graduated from high school and enrolled in college. He also got involved in filmmaking as an actor and scriptwriter.

THINK ABOUT IT

Moving always means leaving something behind—often something we will miss dearly. Is it better to stay in one place to avoid the pain of that loss, or forge ahead to new experiences? Why?

Do you have one childhood crush or romance that stands out in your memory? How did it turn out?

MY MOTHER'S GIFT

BY RAELLE CHARLES

I lost my first set of gold jewelry, which included a Scorpio ring (my Zodiac sign). My mother swore she would never buy me any jewelry ever again. But she changed her mind two years later, when I turned 10. Maybe she felt sympathy for me since I was so upset after losing that first set. She also knew that I was older and could take better care of my things, so she bought me a new pair of gold earrings.

They were hoops about the size of a quarter, with different colored stones on the hoops. They were just the right size for my face, and they went with me everywhere—to church, the beach, the movies, and school.

For years, those gold earrings were the only jewelry I ever wore. They were the only piece of my mother with me in Haiti when she went to the U.S. to go to college.

Raelle's mother gives her a pair of gold earrings as a keepsake, but she loses them when she comes to the United States.

My earrings made me feel beautiful. Once I forgot to wear them to a birthday party, and I felt like I was missing something.

When I started high school in this country, the first person who talked to me complimented me on my earrings and made me feel pretty. I don't know if he was looking for a way to meet me, but it worked.

I remember when I was in 10th grade, getting ready for a Valentine's Day party at school. I switched earrings to match the color of my outfit, which was rare for me since my gold earrings matched all of my outfits.

I thought I had put the earrings in my bag. But when I got home later that day, I searched my bag and couldn't find them. At that moment, I knew that I would never get them back. But the next morning, I still went to school early and looked for them. I asked the janitor more than 20 times over the next week if she'd seen the earrings and she always said no.

> **THOSE GOLD EARRINGS WERE THE ONLY PIECES OF MY MOTHER WITH ME IN HAITI.**

I hid my loss from my mother for a long time. Finally, one day several weeks later, she asked me where my earrings were. I tried to make it seem like nothing. I told her I had put them somewhere and I'd forgotten where, but she kept bugging me so I told her what had happened.

She was mad, and so was I. I loved those earrings so much and because of my irresponsibility, I lost them. Years of memory were gone in a flash. I was upset but I didn't want to accuse anybody of stealing. So I had to live with the fact that I had lost a fortune, something I'd hoped I could cherish forever.

I had been thinking about passing my earrings on to my future daughter when she reached the age I'd been when my mother had given them to me. It would have been a tradition started by me for the rest of my family to come.

Since then, I've never bought or worn another pair of gold earrings. I want it to be a special day when I receive my next pair, hopefully from someone special. But I don't think I will ever value them more than my lost pair. The new earrings will never be the ones I received from my mother back in Haiti when I was only 10 years old.

Raelle graduated from high school and enrolled in the City College of New York.

THINK ABOUT IT

Do you keep a special memento or object from someone you love? What is it and why is it important to you?

Do you have a special object or possession that you would like to pass down to your children or a loved one? What would you like them to get out of your gift?

Why might a keepsake be especially important to someone who has moved to another country?

V. Hard Transitions

I Showed My Enemies, and Hurt My Friends Too

By Elie Elius

(Some names have been changed.)

When I came to America from Haiti, I was very shy and passive. I was the new kid on the block and I was desperate to be liked. The best way I could make friends, I thought, was to fit in with the crowd. I used to let my so-called friends walk all over me because I was afraid that if I spoke up, they wouldn't want to be seen with me.

They told me I was down and I could hang with them, but later on I found out they were using me as a big joke. Phrases

Elie, a shy and passive boy, is bullied and teased when he comes to America, and it has an impact on him throughout his youth. Only when he gets to high school does he finally become comfortable in his new country, and more importantly, in his own skin.

like, "You hear the way that guy talks!" or, "He looks so ugly and retarded," were constantly being thrown at me.

I did not know English well and people would make fun of the way I spoke. Their words would sizzle on my skin like butter hitting a hot skillet. Plus, back in the day, my head used to be bigger than my body and a person couldn't tell me from a brown toothpick. All of these flaws added up to laughter and jokes at my expense.

Just for the hell of it, one of my friends would say, "Your father left you 'cause he didn't want your ugly ass." My father, a deadbeat, left my mother before I was born, and my so-called friend had no idea why he flew out on us. Still, just hearing him say those words made me feel hurt and angry.

I felt their words strike my heart like a sharp, pointy spear. I felt like dirt under their shoes that they could just wipe off. And, from around the time I was 9 'til I was about 12, it went on and on. But then I began to decide that enough was enough.

No, I didn't wake up one morning and say, "OK, no more." But slowly, as I got older, I decided that I was tired of coming home from school crying. I was sick of avoiding my cousins, who also made fun of me, and hiding out in the kitchen if they were in the living room.

Reader, what would you do if you were constantly being picked on?

When I talked to people I was close to, they would say, "Pay them jerks no mind. Keep your head up at all times." When I came home depressed, my mother would sometimes say, "People picked on me all the time. Just ignore their talk."

But I could not ignore it and I did not know how to keep my head up. If I wanted this foul treatment to stop I would either have to A) run away, 'cause I knew my mother would not move just because I was getting picked on, or B) change my attitude and start wiping people off of me.

By my own popular demand, I chose B.

Change is a hard path to cross in life. Sometimes it is for the better, sometimes it is for the worse. Who really knows? Maybe the person who is doing the morphing does not know himself.

The good point for me was that I let a lot of people know I was not going to take their crap. The bad point was that I lost a lot of good people by being too hard. Still, the first time I really stood up for myself took a lot of courage, and I'm glad I did it.

One day, a kid went up to the board when the teacher was not there and drew me as a stick figure with mean little details. One of my so-called friends found this so amusing he just had to join in. The whole class was laughing and pointing at me, and I felt like a rag.

I DID NOT KNOW ENGLISH WELL AND PEOPLE WOULD MAKE FUN OF THE WAY I SPOKE.

At first I just went up and asked them if they could stop making fun of me because I didn't like it. Then my friend began to mock me and the other kid pushed me.

I went back to my seat but they were still up there laughing, and the other kids were pointing and laughing also. At that moment I couldn't take it. I remembered my uncle saying that if you want to get through to people, you have to be aggressive. So I stood up, walked to the front of the class, and erased my picture.

Where on earth did that courage come from? I have no idea but I'm glad it came.

"What the hell is your problem?" the kid asked me. I cursed at him.

It was right there and then I got into my first fight. My friend punched me in the face and the other kid punched me in the stomach. Even though I lost, this incident began the whole "Don't mess with me" sitcom. After that, I began to be more and more aggressive.

Day by day, my tormentors began to recede as I gradually became more foul-mouthed and increasingly got into fights. People stopped picking on me and I had this feeling that I had accomplished something big. The problem was that in some ways, I began to act different with just about everybody—not just my so-called friends, but my real friends, too.

At any little thing someone did to me, even if it was just a friendly joke, I would snap or get ready to fight. Lots of times when I probably didn't need to, I kept my distance and had my guard up. Plus, if I was hurt, I wouldn't talk to my friends about what was going on. I'd cut them out or get into a fight. That's how I lost my friend Syretta.

Syretta was one of my best and most trusted friends. But for her 13th birthday, she invited some friends to her house for her party and didn't invite me. I did not want to go up to her and ask her what was going on because I felt embarrassed. So I went uninvited. When I saw my friend Rafael, I went over to talk to him about Syretta.

"You know that fat pig did not invite me," I said. "What she got with me anyway?"

I guess someone overheard what I said because a couple of minutes later Syretta's mother was in my face.

"I will really appreciate it if you would leave my home," she said. "I do not like or allow this kind of rudeness in my house."

I was so outraged that I actually went up to Rafael and punched him because I thought he was the one who told Syretta what I said. When I did this, everyone stopped and looked at me with disgust. Syretta's father called my mother. Then he dragged me out of his house.

At the time I was just angry. But now I feel ashamed. I was cursing and carrying on like I had no type of home training. And I feel bad, because even though I was hurt about the party, Syretta had been good to me and I messed up our friendship. Sometimes I still regret the way I carried myself. I do believe it's important to stand up for yourself, but all that big and bad stuff wasn't me.

Times change and so do people. When I went into high school, I decided I had to act and carry myself differently. I decided that when I entered the school building, I entered for an education, not to be liked. At first I stuck by myself. But soon I found that people were coming up to me and wanting to be my friend, probably because I was just being myself.

Now, if I have a problem or conflict, most often I will try to talk things through. I know who my real friends are—they're the ones who give me respect—and I know more about who I am too. I am not a punk, and no matter what people say or do, I don't want to go to extremes fighting anymore.

Elie was in high school when he wrote this story.

THINK ABOUT IT

In reaction to being teased as a new immigrant, Elie decided to fight back with his fists and mouth. Did that approach work for him? Why or why not?

When Elie is teased, some of his friends join in. How might the situation had been different if instead of joining in, they had stood up for him? Does a bystander have any responsibility to step in and try to stop things if someone is being mistreated? Why or why not?

If he has a problem or conflict now, Elie says he talks it through. Why do you think he has been able to change?

STICK WITH YOUR OWN KIND?

BY CASSANDRA THADAL

Here's a scene from a typical day in my high school classroom: students from various countries, such as Mexico, Poland, Bangladesh, Yemen, and the Dominican Republic are talking and laughing as they work together and help each other.

The teacher yells, "Why am I hearing you talking? Shouldn't you be working?"

"We work and talk at the same time," we answer.

When the clock marks lunchtime, we run eagerly out of our classroom and head for the cafeteria. But by the time we reach our destination, the kids who mixed happily in the classroom have left that spirit of unity behind.

At most of the tables in the cafeteria, you see faces of the same

Cassandra's high school is diverse and the students mingle freely in class. But in the cafeteria, they rarely mix. Cassandra feels pressure to stick with her fellow Haitians, but defies the pressure and develops friendships with teens from many backgrounds.

color. The students enjoy this time with their own folks. The kids say they do this because it's just more comfortable. So whoever arrives in the cafeteria first gets her food and spots some seats, then saves a place for others of her same race or ethnic group.

After lunch, they leave together and spend the rest of the period in the hallways, or outside if it's not cold. A group of Polish kids settles on the floor near the main office, chatting and gossiping. Sometimes other Polish kids play checkers or dice nearby.

Some of the Dominicans sit in the hallway a few feet from the Polish kids. Most of the time they talk loudly and sing in Spanish or dance. A little further, along some kids from Ecuador or Peru hang out. The Bengalis gather in one classroom, listening to Bengali music. The Haitian girls—the group I am part of— hang out next to our counselor's office, while the Haitian boys assemble on the stairs.

The students are allowed to roam around freely like this because my school is very small and generally there's harmony. People may have their personal

AT MOST TABLES IN THE CAFETERIA, YOU SEE FACES OF THE SAME COLOR.

disagreements, but groups rarely fight. That doesn't mean that everybody's friends, though—they aren't. They generally stick with their own kind.

Of course, some teens do befriend people from different races. One Polish girl often hangs with a Filipina girl, and there are two black guys, one from France, the other from Africa, who are friends with a kid from Mexico. I am also someone who doesn't stick only to my own race—although this wasn't always the case. When I first arrived here I had never spent any time with white people.

I lived in Haiti until I was 14. When I saw white people in Haiti, I hated them because I knew that whites had enslaved and mistreated blacks. I didn't know any whites who considered blacks equal. Also, some Haitians have the annoying habit of saying, "Oh, the whites are so smart!" whenever they saw great things like computers or cars, as if no black person could invent things, and I hated that.

When I moved to the U.S., I began to experience being around people of other races. I sat in a classroom and saw all different kinds of people. I wanted to talk to them—except the whites. My friends were Chinese, Honduran, and Haitian. But when I saw the white kids, I said to myself, "I am not going to talk to these people." I assumed they were saying the same thing because I'm black. But gradually my attitude changed.

The white kids at school treated me nicely, and I saw that many blacks were doing great at my school. It seemed like in the U.S., whether you're black or white, you can do great things. In class I learned that we all had things in common and I began to feel comfortable. My friends and I often discussed racism. We thought that teenagers should mix. Our culture and skin color differed, but in the classroom we ignored our differences and got along very well.

So it surprised me that when I returned to school last fall, I stopped mingling with other races and stayed with two Haitian girls. It didn't happen that way because I was being a racist, or at least I didn't think so.

It was because my Honduran friend, Daysa, was not yet back from vacation, and most of my old Chinese friends were in other classes. So every day during lunch, I started sitting with the Haitian girls.

After Daysa came back, I still spent most of my time with the Haitians. Daysa spoke with her friends in Spanish and I spoke Haitian Creole with my friends. I didn't see any problem with this until one day I got to the lunchroom before my two Haitian friends.

A friend of mine from the Dominican Republic asked me to

sit with her, so I did. When my Haitian friends came, they looked at me strangely, but I didn't react and just said, "Hi." Then I ate my lunch and talked to the Dominican girl.

Later, when my Haitian friends were leaving, they passed and said, "Oh, yeah, Cassandra, you're buying the Spanish face." ("Buying someone's face" is a Haitian expression. It means you are sucking up to someone from a position of inferiority.

I laughed and said, "What do you mean I'm buying the Spanish face? Sitting with someone Spanish has nothing to do with that." Later I talked with one of my friends and told her that what they said wasn't fair and didn't make me happy.

"OK, girl," she said, and that was it. We were again at peace.

WE NEED TO BREAK DOWN THE WALLS IF WE WANT RACISM TO STOP.

Later in the year, I became friends with a Russian girl named Natasha. We were in the same group in class and she was very nice to me. We always talked to each other in class and she often called me on the telephone, but we never sat together at lunch.

One day my Haitian friends were sitting at our table while I was still standing in line. After I got my meal I saw Natasha and she called to me.

"Come sit with me!"

"Oh...I'm sorry. I have to sit with the Haitians or else they'll say that I'm buying your face. You know..."

"What?" Natasha said, confused. I explained the expression and she said, "OK, I'll see you later."

I left her by herself and went to my other friends. Because I didn't want my Haitian friends to tease me, I stopped hanging out with people of other races.

Sometimes in the morning I still walked around with one of the Chinese guys who had been my friend since 9th grade. My friends from Haiti never said anything about that, but another

Haitian girl told me, "Cassandra, you love the Chinese too much. You're buying their faces."

I laughed and told her she was wrong. Still, I confined my friendships with kids from other races to the classroom, because I hated what my Haitian friends said whenever I hung out with them at lunch.

The Haitian students mean a lot to me and I always try to get along with them because they're my people. I never told them how much I was bothered by what they said. Then I started to write this story, and I began to think about how we were all acting.

I realized I had become a different person by not mixing with other students when I wanted to. And when I realized that, I decided to change back to who I really am.

Now, in the cafeteria, I sit with Natasha, my Russian friend, along with my Honduran friend, Daysa.

I had stopped mixing with other kids because I was scared of what my friends would think and say. It's good to stay with "your people" sometimes. But, at the same time, if you only stay with your people, you're missing out on a lot of opportunities to make new friends and have new experiences.

We need to break down the walls of language, culture, and skin color if we want racism to stop. We share many common things, but the only way we can find out what they are is if we mix.

Cassandra graduated from high school and attended college.

THINK ABOUT IT

In your school, do kids of different races, nationalities, or backgrounds mix together or stay separate? Why do you think kids sometimes prefer to "stick to their own kind"?

The next time you are in the cafeteria, take a look around at who is sitting with who. Imagine that the school has decided that every Monday students will be assigned random seating in the cafeteria. Almost everyone will be seated with people they don't know well and the goal is to get students to know people they don't otherwise talk to. The principal has asked for suggestions for how to make this new arrangement work. Give her some advice.

FIGHTS IN AMERICAN SCHOOLS FREAKED ME OUT

BY SABRINA RENCHER

(Some names have been changed.)

I'm originally from Haiti and lived there until I was 12. The schools I attended there were orderly and peaceful, as opposed to what I've experienced in New York City schools.

Here, I've seen students fighting and cursing each other like it was no big deal. That freaked me out when I first arrived.

Between the ages of 2 and 5, I attended a private school in Haiti. There I learned to never hit or curse at my teachers or other kids and to do my homework and study. When I started elementary school at the College Saint Louis de Bourdon, these rules became even more important. Since we were older, the teachers

> *In Haiti, students are deeply respectful toward teachers and are well-behaved at school. The fighting and disrespect in American schools are a shock for Sabrina.*

there had higher expectations and were stricter than our instructors in kindergarten.

"The things that we learn today are the things that we are going to use tomorrow," one teacher told my class.

Growing up, that philosophy became a big part of who I am. Without it, I don't think I would have had the focus to finish high school and go on to college.

In Haiti, I liked being the careful and well-behaved Sabrina. I got positive feedback for following adults' instructions and caring about my future. My teachers gave me compliments for being quiet in class and always doing my homework. They called my mother in just to tell her how well I was doing.

But there were times when my school's rules felt overwhelming. Students who didn't follow our school's code got punished by their parents and teacher. That was a lot of pressure.

> **I REALIZED I PREFER HAVING STRICT RULES TO GUIDE ME.**

I sometimes felt like a slave because I didn't feel free to mess up, particularly after seeing what happened to Stacie, a girl who cursed out one of our teachers.

The principal was upset because of the example Stacie set for the younger kids and wanted to expel her, but her mother begged for a second chance. The principal gave it to her. So Stacie got suspended for two days. She told us her mother beat her for getting in trouble and talked all day about how, if she was kicked out of this school, she'd be barred from other schools.

Even though the incident with Stacie may not seem like a big deal, she was the only student I ever knew who got into major trouble in Haiti. And her example was enough for me.

My oldest cousin, Guerdy, who was a teenager, told me that students in higher grades had to be even more respectful. She said she knew a girl who got kicked out of school for doing the same thing Stacie did. Unlike Stacie, she wasn't allowed to come back because she was older and considered mature enough to know wrong from right.

Even though I was generally comfortable back in Haiti, by the time I was 11 my mother wanted us to go to America, partly for my education and safety. A lot was going on in Haiti at the time. For example, many workers were protesting low salaries, including teachers, and their boycotts sometimes caused me to miss school.

People were also unhappy with Haiti's government. [The president had been forced out of the country by a military coup. see Timeline, p. 120.] There was violence in the streets because of the political unrest. Even though I felt safe at school, the country was not stable. My mother thought if I stayed in Haiti, I'd fall behind in my learning because of the boycotts. She wanted me to finish school when I was supposed to and have the career I wanted.

When I knew I was coming to the United States, I expected that I'd have to adjust to a different educational system. I just didn't realize how rough it would be.

My first year in America, I attended a middle school where some kids were all about breaking the rules. They cut classes to hang out with their friends like it was nothing. One time, some people asked me to cut school; there would be two other girls and three boys. They were thinking about having a make-out party.

I said, "No thanks." I didn't want to do that because if caught, I could've ended up suspended and in trouble with my mom. In Haiti, I wouldn't even have had the option to cut school because there the school doors are closed once you're in school and no one is allowed out until dismissal. I realized I prefer having strict rules to guide me; otherwise, I might slack off.

But having more freedom to cut class wasn't nearly as traumatic as watching kids fight. In 7th grade, two gangs went at it after a member of one gang looked at a member of a rival gang wrong. Two guys told other gang members, and soon there was a gathering of thugs in the yard. These two guys got into each other's face and started cursing each other out.

I watched from a doorway. Fists flew everywhere. So many boys were fighting, I couldn't keep count. Most of them got suspended for fighting on school property.

After the fight, I was frightened because I thought, "What if someone started a fight with me?" I didn't go to school the next day because I was scared.

It wasn't just boys who caused trouble. A set of twin sisters in my school cursed at teachers and students whenever they felt like it. Once, my friend Amy was walking down the hall and one sister bumped into her.

> **SO MANY BOYS WERE FIGHTING, I COULDN'T KEEP COUNT.**

The other twin said, "Why did you push my sister and didn't even tell her sorry?"

"Because she bumped into me," Anne said.

The twin cursed at her. Then Amy cursed her back. One of the sisters jumped on her and punched her in the face. Amy pushed her off and punched her back. The fight ended because a security guard came and stood between them.

I watched the fight from the doorway of my native language class. Some of us tried to jump in because Amy was our friend, but my teacher stopped us. Amy and the twins had to go to the principal's office. But they weren't even suspended. They were all in school the next day. This would've been unheard of in Haiti.

I felt unsafe and worried that some day I might get beaten by some school hooligan. I was also scared that the discipline I learned in Haiti would leave my head and new ideas would creep in, like having sex and being vulgar.

Even though I liked some of the freedom I experienced

here—like having teachers who weren't so strict—I was worried that I'd start acting like someone who doesn't care about her future. So one day as I was eating in my kitchen, I asked my mother, "Mommy, can we go back to Haiti? I don't like the fact that the kids here are always getting in trouble."

"If you go, you will be going alone," she said.

I didn't want to stay here, but I didn't want to go back to Haiti without my mom. So I said, "Fine. I'll stay." But I was angry at her for making me stay in the middle of all these school fights.

For about a year, I kept asking her if we could go back. She said that we would in a matter of time. After a while, though, I got used to the idea of staying here and learning new things. As I finished junior high, I thought more about the opportunities that this country has to offer.

My mother explained that there are more jobs available here than in Haiti for people who graduate from college. She also explained that there are more scholarships, grants, and loans available for students here to make education more affordable. Plus, my education here hasn't been interrupted by boycotts or violence in the streets like it was back home.

I also realized that my fears were made larger because I hadn't felt that connected to people.

I'm now a sophomore in high school and I've grown more accustomed to New York school culture. The school I'm in now feels calmer than my junior high because there isn't as much fighting and the students are friendlier with each other. Still, I feel I'm more willing to get into fights after being here for four years.

One day I argued with my mother before school, so I was in a bad mood. Then a Haitian girl came up to me in chemistry class and accused me of talking about her. She said, "If you ever talk about me, you won't go home with your mouth." I was so enraged that I attempted to jump on her, but some boy held me back.

After the incident my chemistry teacher, Mr. Rousselin, gave me a long speech. "We're supposed to be setting an example," he said. He is also Haitian and believes Haitian students should stick together. A part of me agreed with what he was saying, but part of me didn't because I was still angry. Still, I realized that I should have found a better way to handle my anger.

Despite having to deal with school violence, I've made up my mind to make New York my home and take advantage of its opportunities. I plan to become a pediatrician. I told my mother I'm giving New York a chance, even though I still think that the kids here have too much freedom. I will go back to Haiti, just not that soon. After all, I have school to think about.

Sabrina graduated from high school and went to college in New Jersey.

THINK ABOUT IT

How does Sabrina describe schools in Haiti? Do you think you would prefer attending a school with such strict rules?

What problems did Sabrina have with her school in the U.S.? Do you think she would have had the same problems in the school you attend? Why or why not?

Sabrina is more willing to fight after becoming accustomed to the culture of New York schools. Do you think your attitude is shaped by the culture of your school? How so?

VI. CHANGING TRADITIONS

DATING, BLACK MAGIC, AND OTHER CHANGES IN AMERICA

BY CLAUDE FRAVIEN

I was born and raised in Haiti. I came to this country about three years ago and I think the experience has been for the best.

When I first came here I hated the country. I wanted to go back to Haiti even though things were pretty bad there: The same year my family left the country the people overthrew "Baby Doc," the country's ruling dictator. That was when the real violence started. (See Timeline, p. 120.)

However, being in America brought its own problems. It meant adjusting to a whole different culture, language, and a new way of life. But I think it's my parents who really need to do the adjusting.

My parents, like a lot of Haitian parents, were afraid of

Claude moves to America as a teen and feels that everything is different, from religious practices, to attitudes about dating, to how teens and parents talk with each other.

spiritual harm. In Haiti, many people fear voodoo (actually black magic) as a potential source of harm. (Voodoo is a religion that combines the religions African slaves carried with them to the New World with the Roman Catholicism of their former masters. See "About Voodoo," p. 132.)

Because black magic is practiced in the U.S. as well as in Haiti, our move here did nothing to alleviate my parents' fears or worry for me. So they counseled me to be careful and to make as few friends as possible. (See "I Still Fear for My Family" on p. 90.)

My parents did not even give me a chance to get close to my peers here. Instead they enforced a strict set of rules.

For example, they wouldn't let me wear certain clothes. According to them, black Americans were all delinquents and they wanted me to avoid any trend or fashion that would help me assimilate with them. When I went to the barber I wouldn't dare get a stylish haircut, because I knew how my parents would react. I knew they'd probably tell me to get a new haircut. And they referred to rap as "bum music."

My parents also don't think that a boy and a girl can have anything but a sexual relationship. And at my age, they think that I'm too young to have a girlfriend.

THEY THINK THAT I'M TOO YOUNG TO HAVE A GIRLFRIEND.

I define a girlfriend as someone you can talk to, someone who is understanding or at least willing to listen, someone who cares, and someone who loves you. My parents define a girlfriend as "someone you sleep with."

So you can see what would happen if I ever tried to tell my father about a girl I had met and liked: Sex would be the first thing that would pop into his head and he would warn me against it. That would be the end of the discussion.

I hated being told what to do and what not to do, but I never told my parents how I felt.

In Haiti, kids may not and cannot talk back to grownups. So far I have never met one Haitian teenager who thinks of his parents as friends. I'm not trying to say that all Haitian parents are like mine, but there wasn't a time when I lived in Haiti that I had fun or enjoyed being alive.

Things only got worse here. It came to a point where I ran away from home. I loved my parents and my sisters and brother, but I'd just had it with the Haitian way of life. I stayed over at my friend's house for the weekend. My parents were worried sick about me and after that they understood some of what I was going through. They changed a little, but things are still pretty bad.

> **NOT ONE HAITIAN TEENAGER THINKS OF HIS PARENTS AS FRIENDS.**

Sometimes I think that my parents don't care about me and that the only reason they feed and shelter me is because they feel they have to. My parents don't take interest in my schoolwork. I try to keep my average around an 85, but my parents never notice. I was promoted to editor of my school newspaper about six months ago, but I think my parents still don't know about it.

I wish that they would tell me sometimes that they're proud of me. When something good happens to me I don't even bother telling them about it, because I know it doesn't make a difference to them. It's like they expect the worst of me.

My parents have never encouraged me to do anything I want to do. For example, I love to write and I want to be a writer or a journalist. But my parents think that journalism is a dangerous field because in Haiti journalists get killed. I try telling them that in the U.S. people have freedom of speech, but it doesn't seem to get into their heads. Every day we have the same argument and I just get tired of it.

Being here has changed my whole perspective on life. My

life took a really sharp turn after I started going to high school. I made a lot of new friends and met nice teachers.

I met Mr. Mulqueen, a student advisor at my school, and whether he realizes it or not, he's been like a father and a friend to me. I go to him when I need help or when I just want somebody to talk to.

The United States is where my real life started. I hope I'll stay here always—and just maybe one day my parents will "wake up and smell the roses."

Claude graduated from high school and college, later working in finance and at a university.

THINK ABOUT IT

If you could give Claude some advice about having a better relationship with his parents, what would you tell him?

Are you as close to your parents/guardians as you would like to be? What would bring you closer?

Is there someone like Mr. Mulqueen in your life—an adult who you can talk to? Who is it?

A HAITIAN-AMERICAN CHRISTMAS: CREMACE AND CREOLE THEATRE

By Edwidge Danticat

For Haitians living in America, Christmas is a time when our two cultures unite in a beautiful and harmonious way.

On Christmas Eve we flock to the nearest church, both to be with others and to celebrate the birth of Christ. On Christmas morning we open our presents, like most Americans, except that the younger family members believe that Santa Claus has left their presents near their beds. After they find them, they bring them to the Christmas tree, where they are opened under flashing lights. Over the several days prior to Christmas, this tree has been decorated by various family members.

Christmas day is spent preparing Christmas dinner while we listen to a number of favorite Christmas songs: "Silent Night," "I'm Dreaming of a White Christmas," and "Papa Noel."

On Christmas night our family shares a meal of brown rice and peas, stuffed turkey, and fried vegetables. The young people in the family are allowed only a small amount of Cremace, the traditional drink that is made up of rum, beer, and coconut juice.

The rest of the evening is spent doing whatever our hearts desire. The elder members of the family may go to a play spoken in Creole, our native tongue, while the younger ones usually go to a disco or a party. Some families, however, spend Christmas night in church praying that God will be lenient toward the world and all of its problems.

Edwidge graduated from high school and college and became a writer.

THINK ABOUT IT

What are your family's holiday traditions? Do you combine two cultures, like Edwidge's family does? Do you have any traditions specific to your family?

Is anything about the celebration Edwidge describes similar to your family's holiday celebration? What is different?

I STILL FEAR FOR MY FAMILY

BY DAVID ETIENNE

A few weeks before I left my home in Haiti to move to New York, my mother woke up early to go pray in front of the local Christian church with a group of other churchgoers. Everyone else in the house was sleeping, and it was still dark outside.

When she got back two hours later, she noticed that our house was surrounded by white powder. Right in front of the door was a basket with a dressed rum bottle, some candles, and a little doll with a lot of big needles on it.

My mother was alarmed because she knew that all of these things symbolize voodoo. Or more properly *wanga*. Voodoo is a popular faith in Haiti and its followers believe in god as well as lesser deities or spirits. (See "About Voodoo," p. 132.) *Wanga* is

David's family is relatively well off in Haiti, and some members even flaunt it. Some other people in their community are resentful, and use voodoo or wanga, to let David's family know their feelings.

when somebody uses spirit worship for bad. Some people call it black magic and say it is the dark side of voodoo, but most followers of voodoo do not practice black magic. Black magic is scary. Because of it many kids in Haiti are so scared to go outside after dark that they don't stop wetting the bed until very late. (While some Haitians are lucky enough to have a toilet in the house, most families have theirs outdoors.)

WE'VE BECOME A TARGET FOR SOME LESS FORTUNATE PEOPLE.

The powder my mother found around our house is used to give people's feet an infection that can be fatal. The dressed bottle is used to capture people's souls, while the doll is to take their souls away from them. To protect our house from spiritual harm, my mother washed the powder off the ground with water. She took some gasoline and spread it over the basket, then used a lighter to burn the basket. By burning it, she was burning everything it represented. While the basket burned, she prayed and circled the house.

The next day she told my two older brothers what had happened, but I was only 12 and they knew I would get scared easily. So they didn't tell me until after I left for the U.S. with my two older sisters, one of my older brothers, and my cousin a few weeks later.

When I left, I cried because I knew I'd miss everyone I was close to. But if I'd known about the black magic symbols my mother had found, I would have cried even more thinking about how my family was in danger. My family is a little more comfortable than most families we know in Haiti. Many of us have been able to go live in America, and this makes people jealous, so we've become a target for some less fortunate people.

It doesn't help that some members of my family love to show off by building the biggest and brightest house in a poor community, or by having party after party just to amuse themselves.

People in Haiti really don't like that, especially when they're struggling. So I know the some people with less won't stop trying to harm us.

The more I've heard about black magic over time, the more terrified of it I've become. A cousin who practices voodoo once told me that people have the power to use black magic to turn people into animals. People in my town said a thief who was passing through once turned himself into a goat to avoid getting caught. And another cousin told me that he was once almost "eaten" by people who practice black magic. By that he meant, he was almost turned into a zombie, a slave into eternity.

Stories like these make me really scared when I think that people want to use black magic to do my family wrong. My family has worked hard for everything we have, but we feel as if everyone wants what we have. So it's hard for us to know who our friends are.

There's no question that I feel safer here in the U.S. In this country, I live my life as if I've never heard about voodoo or *wanga*. Some people say that the spirits can follow you everywhere, but that doesn't bother me because life feels so different here. For example, with the electricity here it's not so dark at night and I go out and come back any time I want. And when I step out of my house, I don't have to look down before I put my foot on the ground.

Waking up every morning and not having to think about black magic or hear a story about it is wonderful. But knowing that the rest of my family is still living back in Haiti worries me. I don't pray very often, but every time I do I make sure to ask God to look after my family there.

David Etienne graduated from high school and enrolled in college. He also got involved in filmmaking as an actor and scriptwriter.

THINK ABOUT IT

David fears for family he left behind. Does your family or a family you know have relatives they worry about in their home countries? Why are they worried?

Voodoo, Wanga, black magic, and zombies: Holy Cow! What was strange about David's story for you? Was there anything you could relate to? What are some of the things that you are afraid of? Why are you afraid of them?

I WANTED TO BE PRETTY AND POPULAR

BY SABRINA RENCHER

As a freshman, I thought that I wasn't beautiful enough for people to like me at my high school. That was difficult to deal with because I wanted to be popular.

I'm originally from Haiti. There, I felt gorgeous. I felt as if I didn't have to do anything to fit in with people at school. We had to wear uniforms, which meant we didn't worry about who was more stylish. I didn't have to worry about being popular because I'd spent six years in the same school and more than enough students knew who I was.

But once I arrived here at age 11, I began to feel insecure. My cousin would talk about stars like Mariah Carey and Jennifer Lopez, saying how beautiful they were and that she wished she had their kind of body.

Standards of fashion and beauty are different in America. Sabrina struggles to make sense of them and find her place.

Back in Haiti, girls my age didn't really go on about the bodies of stars. But after listening to my cousin, I began to think about how I looked. I wasn't sure if I was as sexy or beautiful as these stars. I also felt insecure because my cousin was smaller than me, which was devastating. I wanted to have the same kind of body she and her friends had.

Sometimes when I looked in the mirror, I saw one of the ugliest girls in the world. Ever since I was little, I'd been getting bumps on my face from eating peanut butter and chocolate. My doctor said it was an allergic reaction. I tried to stop eating these foods but I couldn't help myself. When I had these bumps, my mother sometimes said that my face looked ugly, which made me sad. It hurt my feelings to hear that from my mother.

My looks were still an issue when I started 9th grade. But instead of wanting to have my cousin's body now, I wanted to look like the Spanish-speaking girls in my school. I thought they were beautiful.

At my high school around half of the students are Latina. It was mostly the Latina girls who wore very tight pants, and some had belly-showing shirts. Many of the other girls covered their bodies, particularly if they were Muslim.

I thought the Latina girls' styles made them look very sexy. Some of them had the body that I dreamed of having. They had almost the perfect butt and chest size. They had slim hips and beautiful faces. Their hair was longer than mine and looked soft. Some of them also liked to wear lipstick and eye shadow. Since I didn't feel beautiful, I wanted to have their look.

A particular set of Latina girls was well known in the school. When I first saw them, I thought that they were popular only because of their style and because they had the attitude of girls who like to have fun. And since they were the most beautiful in the school in my eyes, I thought that the only way a girl could be popular was if she was that pretty too. I didn't realize the other reason for the Latina girls' popularity was because the school was mostly Spanish speaking.

I envied them. I was jealous because I wanted to be surrounded by so many friends. I was already friends with some Haitian girls I'd known from junior high. But some of them would talk about me behind my back and create drama. So I felt I'd be happier if I made new friends.

I wanted to befriend the Latina crew. I wanted to get to know them not only because of their looks and popularity, but because they were older and seemed to treat each other with respect. (Of course, I had no way of really knowing this.) I wanted to be one of them so much that I decided not to eat some of the things that I knew could make me gain weight, like McDonald's, pizza, or any other junk food, for a whole month. I also stayed away from peanut butter and chocolate to prevent the bumps.

I'M ORIGINALLY FROM HAITI. THERE, I FELT GORGEOUS.

I started going to a gym near my house to work out every weekend. Then one day, a month after I started to go to the gym, I made another change. I bought lipstick, eye shadow, face powder, lip liners, and eyeliners. I went home and gave myself a makeover. I put on my tight jeans and belly-showing t-shirts.

I looked new. I looked like the kind of person lots of people would think of as beautiful. I was satisfied. I started to carry a mirror in my book bag to look at the pretty face that I'd created. That's when I started to call myself "Sabrina the Princess." I felt stronger and more confident.

But my mother didn't like what I'd done to myself. Every time I wore one of my shirts, she said "You are going to wear something over that, right?" I would say "yes," and leave with a shirt closed over my midriff; then, when I got to school, I'd open it.

But I was still the same person, and I didn't like that. I was quiet around anyone I met, so I decided to change my attitude, too. I thought the only way to be popular was to be like the Spanish-speaking kids, who seemed very outgoing.

So I gave my attitude a little touch up and started acting like the popular Latina crew. I started to look tough and walk sexy. Still, not many people talked to me. I did make some new friends because they were in my class. But I wanted to be friends with the most popular Latinas because I wanted everybody in school to know who I was.

I spent the rest of 9th grade trying to connect with those girls. I sometimes sat next to them in English or social studies class. But they would say nothing to me. I tried to start conversations with them by saying "Hi." They said, "Oh, hi." And that was it. I had no clue what would work to get them to acknowledge me.

I was upset and didn't know how to handle my feelings. So my sweet self started to change into the kind of person I would've never wanted to become. I started to not do my homework. I also started to ignore my mother when she was talking to me.

During the summer after 9th grade, I thought a lot about what happened. I remembered when I was 10 and knew I was coming to America. My uncle was worried that I would become too Americanized, so I'd made a promise that I wouldn't change myself for somebody to like me.

WHEN I LOOKED IN THE MIRROR, I SAW ONE OF THE UGLIEST GIRLS IN THE WORLD.

I thought about my promise now as I wrote down my thoughts in my journal. I felt horrible writing about how I was acting because I wasn't listening to my true feelings. But making friends was more important to me than anything else. And I thought to make friends I had to change.

Then one morning in September, before the fall semester started, I turned on the TV and began to watch a talk show. It was about girls who wanted to be popular so badly that they tried to make themselves smaller. They would spend days without eating. Their mothers were worried about them, so they asked the talk show host for help.

The talk show host gave the girls advice that I also needed to hear. He said, "Don't try so hard to be popular in school. If you do want to be popular, just be yourself and if the kids don't like you as you, then they don't deserve your friendship."

That made me think about what I was trying to do. Then I realized that I had to be me, Sabrina, and be happy with who I am and not change myself for anybody. That same day, I wrote in my journal about what the talk show host had said and what it meant to me.

> **I'VE BECOME POPULAR IN SCHOOL BY JUST BEING MYSELF.**

I wrote: "Changing myself to fit in a certain crowd is not what I want to do. My mother always taught me to respect myself and this time I didn't. I disrespected myself by thinking that they'd become my friends if I changed my looks and the way I act. I don't have to change myself for them to like me."

I soon returned to school to start 10th grade. The girls I wanted to be friends with last year were in some of the same classes as me. I decided to show them the real me. The Sabrina who is sweet and funny and doesn't obsess about how she looks.

In math class, for instance, I started helping them by explaining problems they didn't understand. That made it easier for us to start talking about other things (like boys!).

Eventually, as we got to know each other better, we started going to the mall to hang out and buy stuff that we didn't need, like sunglasses and clothes. We soon became good friends.

We now tell each other secrets and help each other with our homework. We laugh at each other's jokes. I feel like I belong and that they're going to be some of my best friends for a long time, no matter where they are.

I've also become popular in school by just being myself. Before, I thought that if the Spanish-speaking crew were my friends, everybody else would know who I was. But I'm pretty well-known among both students and staff members by interacting with them on my own rather than just being automatically known as one of the popular girls. (Doing your work and having a sense of humor helps.)

I still wear makeup and bellybutton showing tops, but not as much as I used to. And I've gone back to eating chocolate and peanut butter despite my bumps. My appearance right now doesn't matter as much to me. I love myself for who I am.

I always go back to read old journal entries. When I get to the page where I wrote about what the talk show host said about changing who you are to fit into the popular crowd, I realize I never want to go back to that planet again.

Sabrina graduated from high school and went to college in New Jersey.

THINK ABOUT IT

What are the differences in how Sabrina feels about herself while in Haiti versus here? Why do you think that is?

Sabrina describes what some teens do to fit in with the popular crowd. What have you done to fit in? What have you seen others do? Did those things work? Why or why not?

MOVING TO THE MUSIC

BY RAELLE CHARLES

I started dancing when I was 10 years old in Haiti, where I was born. I was chosen to dance by the nuns at Immaculée Conception, my Catholic elementary school in Port-au-Prince, Haiti.

As part of the nuns' dance group, I performed a dance called "nymes," which is used in Catholic religious services in Haiti. In nymes, specific dance movements correspond with the words of a song. I think of it as singing, but using movement instead of words. I danced for my faith in God, and it felt very delicate, soothing, and inspirational to me.

We'd dance when it was any nun's birthday, on Christmas, and for special masses and Carnival, in the second week of February. But I didn't just dance for religious ceremonies. As I was growing up, my father taught me a lot of other dances. Salsa, meringue, ballroom—I learned them all. I remember him making

As a girl in Haiti, Raelle loves to express herself through dance. She finds new ways of doing so after moving to America.

me stand on his feet and leading me like a robot.

"You are a fast learner. Good job!" he'd say, whenever I did something right.

I can remember dancing with him after my First Communion in the Catholic Church when I was 10. It was a very special day to me, the day that Christ invited me to eat his flesh (by eating the Communion wafer) and drink his blood (by drinking the Communion wine).

After the church service, my godmother threw me a party at her house. My father and I were the first ones on the dance floor, dancing to kompa music (native Haitian music), which asks the dancers for a lot of passion. It's danced by a duo moving as one. It's a beautiful experience, like when a slow wave of the sea moves you.

SALSA, MERINGUE, BALLROOM—I LEARNED THEM ALL.

I've always thought of my dad as a professional dancer, although he actually works at a school bus company. When I asked him how he taught himself, he'd always say the same thing: "To me dancing is not something that can be taught. It has to come from within you. Just close your eyes and go with the flow, and you will know how to dance."

If I'd had my way, I would have kept dancing in Haiti. But my dancing was cut short when I turned 12 and my father brought us to the U.S., where my mother was already in college studying accounting.

I didn't know if I'd ever get the opportunity to perform again. I was pessimistic because the kind of dance group I had back home didn't exist in the U.S. (People here don't even know what nymes is.)

When I started high school a couple of years ago, I learned that my school didn't have a dance program. But another high school, which is in the same building as my school, has a dance studio near the building's front door. I'd always pass it when the dancers were in class.

I could hear the music and the stomping of their feet while waiting for the elevator and it was too tempting to me. So I talked to the dance director about joining her program. She told me to ask my principal, who gave me permission to take a class there.

I was really happy but also scared. I didn't speak a lot of English yet and I worried about fitting in, since I didn't go to that school. The other dancers treated me fine, but I never could get to class on time, since my school's schedule was different than theirs. I fell behind and it was hard to catch up when everybody was learning something else.

But I still got to dance. Around Christmas, I performed to a hip-hop song with a lot of other students in the school. It was my first time performing in front of a U.S. crowd and I enjoyed it. I also liked learning new dances, like African stepping, hip-hop, and Jamaican reggae.But it was too hard to get to class on time. So after four months I dropped out.

Luckily, I got another chance to dance, this time at my own school. In May of the following year, I heard about our school's annual talent show. I volunteered to sing backup and dance with a friend (and his girlfriend) who writes his own songs and music. We called ourselves "The Diamonds" and wore downtown hip-hop street dance clothes to perform a hip-hop song we called "Hey Y'all."

OUR MOVES WENT PERFECTLY WITH THE TEMPO OF THE SONG.

Our moves went perfectly with the tempo of the song. While we were performing, somebody yelled my name so loudly that I was startled and almost fell off the stage. But the crowd cheered a lot and that made me feel very pleased.

Afterwards, I was surprised by the reactions of my fellow students. Walking down the school hallway, they congratulated us and imitated us by performing our most exotic moves over and over again. I was really proud of all the backbreaking work that we had put in to make this performance successful (two to three hours a day for two months).

I felt so happy dancing for my school. Maybe it was because I was doing it with people that I knew and my friends were there to encourage me and attend the performances. Or maybe it was because of the positive reaction of the kids.

This year I danced at my school's annual international festival, where everybody dances to music from their native countries. We also got to perform to hip-hop music. And I still dance kompa at parties and at home, sometimes with my father. It's part of my culture and I am keeping it.

I'm grateful my father introduced me to dancing, and I hope he can dance all his life. To me, just like my father, it's natural to dance. You just have to go with the flow.

Raelle graduated from high school and enrolled in the City College of New York.

THINK ABOUT IT

Raelle's father taught her a lot about dance. Is there a friend or family member who taught you something that you love to do? What is it?

Raelle is passionate about dance. What are you passionate about? Why?

REWRITING MY DREAM

By Marsha Dupiton

Entering my 1st grade classroom that day felt exhilarating. Everyone had come to school dressed as what they wanted to be when they grew up. Decked out in a custom-tailored lab coat and a pin that said "Dr. Marsha Dupiton," I felt superior to the ballerinas and firefighters gathered inside my classroom. I was shy and usually the last to do anything. But that day I made sure I was first in line to present my future career to my parents and the rest of the world.

When the music was cued, I strutted across the stage and twirled twice to show off my costume. I caught the eye of my mother and heard the cheers of my aunts, and right then and there I was sure of what I wanted to be when I grew up. If I got a standing ovation for dressing up as a doctor, then I would really

Marsha's parents, like many immigrant parents, want her to become a doctor. A career in medicine becomes her dream too— until she realizes that she prefers writing to science.

be celebrated if I actually became one.

I had chosen that costume because of my own doctor. Whenever I went for a checkup, he would use his secret weapon to loosen me up: his Daffy Duck and Bugs Bunny impersonations. He would ask what I was doing in school and was always interested in what I had to say. He seemed so important, yet humble, and I wanted to be just like him. I could imagine helping my patients, young and old, to feel as good as new.

As I got older, I became more serious about my career choice. I took an interest in science experiments and worked hard in science class. My parents quickly latched onto the idea. When anyone asked what I was going to do when I grew up, my family members, close and distant, would say, "Marsha is going to be the family's first doctor."

My parents moved here from Haiti in their early 20s, along with my grandparents, aunts, and uncles, to get a better life for themselves and their future children. My cousins and I were to reap all the benefits of their sacrifices. My father always said to my sister and me, "You're lucky you were born in the United States because you get so many opportunities. Take advantage of it!"

Among my cousins and me, we had a boatload of future professions: a doctor, a lawyer, a pharmacist, and don't forget your traditional nurse. There was so much pressure to become the best.

My science grades weren't Einstein-worthy—at the start of high school, I was getting Cs in science, compared to my As and Bs in other classes. But that didn't stop me from imagining my future as a doctor.

I would have a huge office, three phones that rang off the hook, and a chic condo in Manhattan that I would rarely see because I'd be working and traveling so much. Helping others was still part of my motivation, but I also wanted to be rich and successful and have a job that was practical. Then, one day in the middle of 9th grade, everything changed.

"Marsha? Can you please come see me for a second?" asked Mr. James, my English teacher, during class one day. I looked up from my book, puzzled. Had I heard him right? As far as I knew, a student was only called to the teacher's desk because they were bad or disrupting a class. But I'd done all my work. In fact, our last assignment was one that I'd worked hard on and really enjoyed. I'd written a short story about a girl starting high school for the second time because she moves around a lot.

I got up and slowly approached his desk. Right foot, left foot. Head down. "Yes?" I said. He slid my 10-page story face-down toward me, his face blank as a canvas.

I picked it up quickly to get it over with. My eyes grew wider each time I blinked at the grade in red on my cover page. An A? I'd hoped for a B or even a B+, but an A, that left me speechless.

WRITING MADE ME FEEL FREE.

"Your story was incredible," said Mr. James. "There was a lot of description and it seemed as if I was there. Did you ever think of writing something other than for a grade?"

I shook my head, thinking, "Why would I do that?" Then Mr. James told me he would look for writing programs for me, and that he wanted to display my story on his bulletin board. I was proud that someone had acknowledged my success in one specific thing rather than the general compliments I got on my grades as a whole. For the first time, I was great at something in particular instead of pretty good at everything. I went home that night, pulled an old composition notebook from my bookshelf, and started writing for fun.

Each day I was a different person. On Tuesday I was Jessica, the rich girl who got whatever she wanted, and on Friday I was Nix, a fairy that ruled over her fairy kingdom. Writing all my feelings and thoughts on paper was something entirely different from preparing to become a doctor. Writing made me feel free.

As my English grades continued to shine, I began to imagine what it would be like to be a writer, how it would make me feel happy like it did now. But it seemed far-fetched to me, like a fairy tale job. So I kept my love of writing to myself.

Whenever someone asked what I wanted to be, I still said, "A doctor." But by the middle of junior year, there was no excitement in my voice anymore. I realized that I'd wanted to become a doctor because it symbolized success. I'd been attached to getting the prize, but not the work that was before me for years to come. My dream of becoming a doctor had turned into a roadblock to my passion: writing.

I wanted a career that incorporated writing and informing people about environmental issues. That's when I thought of becoming a journalist. It was like a ready-made job for me. So when I found out about the Youth Communication summer journalism workshop last spring, I eagerly grabbed an application.

> **FOR THE FIRST TIME, I WAS GREAT AT SOMETHING IN PARTICULAR INSTEAD OF PRETTY GOOD AT EVERYTHING.**

Then I sat in my room trying to muster the courage to tell my mother about it. I didn't think my father would mind my change in plans too much, but my mother would be harder to win over. What mother doesn't want to say to her friends that her daughter is a doctor? Finally I picked up the application and walked toward the kitchen, where she was preparing dinner.

"Hey Mommy, I have a thingy to do in the summer with writing. I think it would really help me out senior year," I said quickly. I tried making my face look blank but failed terribly. My eyebrows were raised and my face must have looked like I'd injected a ton of Botox.

She took the application and started to read. I left her to absorb what this application meant not only for my senior year but for my future. I waited nervously in my room until she called me back into the kitchen.

"What is this? You want to be a journalist? What about becoming a doctor? Why would you want a profession that pays so little and has so much competition for jobs?" she said.

"I just really like to write and you know how I've always excelled in English class. This workshop is to improve my writing. If I'm not cut out for it then I'll turn back to becoming a doctor!" I said. But this was a lie. I knew that I would do great in this program. Getting that application was fate.

"You better know what you want; college is around the corner," she said. Her face was drawn and she seemed confused. But she didn't say no.

I walked out of the room feeling that somehow I'd won the battle. I was expecting a bigger confrontation. I'd even prepared a speech in case I had to talk her into letting me do the workshop. I filled out the application right away and put it in my bag.

Later that night I overheard my mother on the phone with my aunts, saying, "Marsha wants to be a journalist now. I just hope she doesn't become like her cousins who bounce between different majors and colleges each year."

I felt frustrated because I'd finally told her about my passion and she didn't fully understand. I've never flip-flopped in my decisions or ideas and I've always been serious about my future.

On the other hand, I understood her concern. She felt that the path to becoming a journalist left much more room to fail than the path to becoming a doctor. And I felt the same way. We were both anxious to see if I was cut out for this highly competitive program.

When I got an acceptance letter from Youth Communication a week later, it was an eye opener for both my mother and me. The fact that I was one of 10 applicants chosen out of 50 reassured my mother that I wasn't going to dive into an occupation that I didn't know I would do well in.

During the writing workshop, my mother did a complete 180. She took an interest in my writing, asking about my day and when my stories were going to get published so she could read them. I feel relieved and happy because it would be a lot harder without her support.

My mother isn't the only one who has changed; I have too. For most of my life I never felt I could do something unpredictable. Becoming a doctor was like a ladder. First college, then medical school, and then a residency. But the paths to becoming a writer are less clear. I'm not sure if there are enough jobs for writers, or whether they pay enough to live comfortably. That felt uneasy to me at first.

For my family, like for many families that emigrated from Caribbean countries to America, unpredictability isn't an option. Our elders made sacrifices to give us the best of everything here, and we're supposed to become successful so we can give back to them and our native country. I still feel that pressure to be the best for my family and for myself.

But it's different this time around. Now that I'm doing something I truly love and know I'll do well in, not just something that puts extra money in my pocket, I feel less pressured and afraid about my choice.

Journalism feels like a more mature and realistic career choice for me than medicine. I consider the steps I'll have to take to become a journalist: my fantasy of life as a doctor didn't include such details. I imagine myself in a college journalism program and on the newspaper and literary magazine staff, eventually becoming editor-in-chief. I see myself getting an internship at NBC or The New York Times. Then my vision speeds to me getting a Pulitzer Prize for environmental journalism.

When I imagine this path, it's filled with adventure and fun because it involves doing something I love. Even though it's not exactly what my family had in mind for me, I feel that journalism is my pathway to my own personal happiness and success. And at the end of the day, that's what matters most.

Marsha graduated from high school and attended the State University of New York at Geneseo.

THINK ABOUT IT

Marsha's idea of success changes in this story. What symbolizes success for you? Has your idea of success changed over time?

Marsha feels pressure from her parents to choose a certain career and be the best. Do you feel this kind of pressure from your parents? Would you like them to be more involved or less involved in your career goals?

VII. HAITI AND THE AMERICAN STORY

WHAT HAPPENED TO MY AMERICAN DREAM?

BY NATALIE NEPTUNE

I was born on January 25, 1981, on a boat traveling from Haiti to America.

When my father first told me I was born in the ocean, I thought I must be a mermaid, and I couldn't understand why I didn't turn into one when I took a bath. Then he explained that I was born on a boat.

My parents came here on that boat in search of a better life. They wanted to leave a country where the police could beat you up for no reason or break into your house, where they raped the women and mutilated the men. As I've grown up, they've told me horror stories of things the police in Haiti have done to their friends. They came to America hoping that things would be different for them and for their children.

Natalie's faith in her newly adopted country is temporarily shaken by police mistreatment of a Haitian man.

Although I've spent my entire life in this country and have never once been to Haiti, officially I am a Haitian citizen. A few months ago, when my parents became American citizens, I decided that I wanted to become one too.

My parents became citizens because of new laws being passed that would cut off or strictly limit aid to non-Americans living in this country. They also thought it would help them bring my older brother, Jean, here to live with us.

> I'VE DECIDED TO WAIT TO BECOME A CITIZEN.

My parents told me that becoming a citizen would help me get money for college. But for me, becoming a citizen seemed like the first step in fulfilling my American dream. I imagined becoming a successful writer and moving out of my neighborhood, where there are so many crackheads and fences everywhere, to someplace with houses and green grass.

But by the time I got my citizenship papers, I had begun to have second thoughts.

Over the summer while I was working at a writing internship, I traveled into Manhattan regularly for the first time in my life, and I began to notice the way black people and other minorities worked in the little jobs—behind the counter or cleaning up the parks—while the white people hurried off to offices in suits and ties. I wondered why almost all the cab drivers were Indian, black, or Middle Eastern, while almost all the passengers were white.

I began to be bothered by the fact that there aren't that many black people in positions of power. I felt angry that politicians want to throw juvenile offenders into adult jails while cutting money out of school budgets. I worried that for minorities like myself, the American dream could turn into an American nightmare.

Then, a few days after I received my citizenship papers, I saw an article in the *Daily News* about a man named Abner Louima who was allegedly beaten and raped with a toilet plunger by cops in New York's 70th precinct. I felt sick to my stomach. The police officers have been given the job of protecting and serving the people of this city, but instead they were trying to kill this man.

The details of the beating and torture were so graphic—by the time Louima was finally taken to the hospital, he had damaged internal organs and broken teeth—that at first I didn't want to read any more. I was so mad I just wanted to see the cops receive the same treatment they had given Louima.

In the evening when I got home, I read the article more carefully: like me, Abner Louima was Haitian.

If he had been African-American or Chinese, I still would have been upset. Any time someone is robbed of his dignity and self-respect, I'm angry. But when I read that he was Haitian and heard on the radio that racist remarks were allegedly made by the police, I was really pissed off. It reminded me of rude things I had heard about Haitians before and I questioned whether I wanted to become a citizen at all.

> **MY PARENTS CAME HERE ON A BOAT IN SEARCH OF A BETTER LIFE.**

In the summer of 1992, a brutal military regime was ruling Haiti and Haitians were fleeing to this country in great numbers. [See Timeline, p. xx.]

Many settled in New York and at that time I heard people in my neighborhood, both black and white, stereotyping Haitians, calling us "boat people," making fun of how we spoke English, and saying that you would get AIDS if you slept with a Haitian woman.

I watched on the news how Haitians—including my own aunt and uncle—were being held prisoner at the Guantanamo

Bay naval base in Cuba in overcrowded conditions just because they were trying to save themselves and seek refuge in America.

When I heard that Louima had been beaten by the police and harassed because he was Haitian, I remembered all these things, and questions filled my mind. Why should I be part of a country that doesn't want to open its arms to people who seek refuge here? Why should I be part of this country if I have to fear the people who are supposed to protect me just like my parents feared the police in Haiti?

Now, I've decided to wait to become a citizen. I guess I feel a little hopeless, and I just don't believe that I can change this country.

I want to become an American citizen for the right reasons—I don't want to do it just so I can get government aid for college or for some other financial benefits. I want to feel passionate about my country and I want to feel like I can bring about change.

Maybe in a few years I'll feel differently. If I do become a citizen, I hope I'll use that power to fight to eliminate some of the problems that I see going on now.

Right now, though, in light of what happened to Abner Louima, I'm just not ready to fill out the forms and declare that I'm part of this country.

Natalie graduated from high school, got a college degree at Vanderbilt University, and eventually decided to become an American citizen.

THINK ABOUT IT

Natalie describes several things that make her have second thoughts about America. What are they? Do you agree with her view? Why or why not?

Have you, or a group you belong to, ever been treated unfairly or stereotyped? In what ways?

A LITTLE PIECE OF HAITI

BY NATALIE NEPTUNE

This summer, I attended a rally in support of Abner Louima and against police brutality. Everywhere people were waving Haitian flags and talking in Haitian Creole.

Before I went to the rally, being Haitian wasn't something that I thought about that much. My mother cooks Haitian food, like blended green plantains. My father listens to Haitian bands, like Phantom or King Posse. Sometimes they'll watch Haitian videos every night of the week because they miss their home so much.

But I've never been to Haiti. When my parents' friends tell me I should speak Creole more, I just want them to get out of my face. After all, I'm in America, not Haiti.

At the rally, though, I was surrounded by Haitian flags and people spoke to me in Creole. There was a middle-aged woman wearing sandals and a white dress with a lot of lace and a pouf at the waist, and it reminded me of the dresses that Haitian mothers make their young daughters wear. The woman was selling candied peanuts, like the kind that my parents bring back when they take a trip to Haiti. I usually eat so much of it that I wind up getting sick.

Having so many Haitian people all around me was a special experience. Being at the rally, I felt that I had found a little piece of Haiti.

THINK ABOUT IT

Do you think a lot about your race or ethnicity? Or is it not that big a deal to you?

HAITI'S PART IN AMERICA'S HISTORY

BY CASSAUNDRA WORRELL

Except for the United States, Haiti is the oldest republic in the Western Hemisphere. It is on the western third of an island, known as Hispaniola, which it shares with the Dominican Republic. It is a place of white sandy beaches, tropical flowers, and political chaos.

Haiti first became a cause for political concern more than 200 years ago when Toussaint L'Ouverture, a slave who taught himself how to read and write, led a successful slave revolt against the French in 1791. That revolt culimated in the birth of the Haitian Republic in 1804.

The Haitian revolution was inspired by the French revolution, which started with the fall of the Bastille in 1789. It was a long and bloody struggle. The French had been brutal slave

The history of Haiti and the United States have intersected in many important ways in the past 220 years.

masters and the island colony was fought over by the major European powers of the day. In the revold led by L'Ouverture, the slaves defeated all these forces. L'Ouverture, sadly, did not live to the decisive victory. In 1802, he was captured and imprisoned in France, where he died in 1803. Jean Jacques Dessalines, another revolutionary leader, was Haiti's first president.

Many Americans were afraid that the slave revolt in Haiti could spread to the U.S. if slaves were aware of what had happened in Haiti. White American slave owners thought Toussaint's empire should be crushed to keep him from "making trouble" in the U.S. As a result, the U.S. did not recognize Haiti as a sovereign state until 1862.

> **EXCEPT FOR THE UNITED STATES, HAITI IS THE OLDEST REPUBLIC IN THE WESTERN HEMISPHERE.**

Despite having been victorious against the French, by the early part of the 20th century, Haiti was disorganized and bankrupt. It could not pay its debts to European nations.

In 1915 the United States sent Marines to occupy Haiti, supposedly to prevent any of Haiti's European debtors from sending in their own forces. The U.S. troops did not leave until 1934, when Haiti had become more socially and economically developed.

The next two presidents encouraged foreign investment in Haiti, but upper class people gained most of the benefits from these investments. Haiti became a country of extreme political unrest. Army officers took control of the government in 1946, and again in 1949 after widespread rioting.

In 1957 a country doctor, Francois Duvalier (nicknamed Papa Doc), was elected president of Haiti. Seven years later he declared himself president for life, and Haiti became a dictatorship.

He changed the country's constitution in 1971 to allow him to choose his successor—his son, Jean-Claude Duvalier. At age

19, Jean Claude (nicknamed "Baby Doc") followed in his father's footsteps and declared himself president for life and ruled as a dictator.

Both father and son controlled the army and a secret police group, the Tonton Macoutes (meaning "bogey-men"), which enforced Duvalier policies through violence. In the early '70s, many Haitians left their country for better living and working conditions and to escape the Tonton Macoutes. A great number fled to the United States.

In 1986, Haitians staged a revolt against Jean-Claude Duvalier. He fled Haiti with his family, in fear of his life.

Editor's Note: Cassaundra wrote this story when she was a teen writer at Youth Communication in 1988. Much has changed in Haiti since then as it has struggled to develop democratic political institutions and faced severe economic challenges. See the following Timeline on the next page for a quick update on Haitian history since 1988.

Cassaundra graduated from high school and college and became a nurse. As an adult, she has participated in medical missions to Haiti.

THINK ABOUT IT

What did you learn about Haiti that you didn't know before? What surprised you the most?

Haiti continues to be poor and chaotic today. What reasons do you see for that?

TIMELINE OF HAITIAN HISTORY

The Colonial Period and Slavery: 1492-1789

During this period Haiti was a colony of Spain (1492-1697) and then France (1697-1789). The native peoples of the island of Hispaniola were virtually wiped and out and replaced with slaves imported from Africa. (Hispaniola is large island in the Caribbean. Present-day Haiti occupies the western third of the island. The Dominican Republic occupies the eastern two-thirds.)

Spain, and then France run brutal slave-based economic systems to generate profits that are sent back to investors in the home countries. Overwork, undernourishment, beatings and torture are normal features of slave life. Wives and husbands and parents and children are separated at the will of the master. Suicide is common; it is believed that death brings not only an end to misery but also a return to Africa.

The Maroons
1700-1758

Bands of runaway slaves, known as the Maroons, began agitating for freedom in the colony in the first forms of revolt. Beginning in 1651, the most famous of the Maroons, Makandal, leads a 6-year rebellion against the slaver owners. He is captured and publicly burned at the stake in 1758.

The Haitian Revolution: 1791-1804

An uprising in August 1791 sparks a long, bloody struggle that culminates in the Haitian Revolution. The call to arms is issued at a Voodoo ceremony, known as the Bois Caiman ceremony. The leader of the ceremony, a Maroon named Bookman, is later captured and executed but the revolt spreads.

Toussaint L'Ouverture (1743-1803) emerges as the most important leader of the revolution.

Early Haiti: The First Black Republic: 1804-1843

On January 1, 1804, 21 years after the American colonists defeat the British to establish the first independent country in the New World, the people of Haiti celebrates their victory over colonial France. It is the first successful slave revolution. The Republic of Haiti is established. Jean Jacques Dessalines becomes the first president.

From 1807-1818, foreshadowing the color conflict that will dominate Haitian society, the country is simultaneously ruled by two leaders, a black man in the North and a mixed race man (mulatto) in the South.

In April 1825, France demands that the newly free country pay 150 million gold francs to French former slave masters to "compensate" for their lost "property." This sum is nearly three times as much as what the French received from the U.S. for Louisiana, an area much larger than Haiti. Haiti is economically and militarily too weak to resist this demand, or to insist that France instead pay reparations for the crimes committed against the slaves. (This crippling debt is not paid off until 1947.)

Political Instability: 1844-1915

Haiti has no less than 22 heads of state in this period. The majority of them are deposed by coup d'états, rebellions and conspiracies.

In 1862, the U.S. finally recognizes Haiti. (Fear of a slave rebellion in the United States had influenced U.S.-Haiti relations ever since the revolution of 1804.)

The U.S. Occupation: 1915-1934

Seeking to protect its investments and interests, the U.S. invades Haiti after the fifth Haitian president in the five years is assassinated. The U.S. dissolves the Haitian legislature, changes the constitution to allow foreigners to own land, reinstates virtual slavery for public works projects, and forms and trains a new Haitian army. An armed rebellion, known as the Cacos Rebellion, is defeated. By the U.S.'s official estimate, more than 3,000 Haitians are killed during this period.

Post-U.S. Occupation: 1934-1956

In October 1937, the Dominican dictator Rafael Trujillo orders the killing of Haitians living on the Dominican side of the border between the two countries. The resulting three days of killing, known as the Parsley Massacre, leave an estimated 10,000 to 20,000 Haitians dead. (The test given to suspected Haitians was whether they could pronounce the Spanish word for parsley.) Trujillo then develops an official ideology and policy of racial discrimination, known as Anti-Haitianismo. Haitians become the scapegoats of Dominican society.

Thirty-Year Duvalier Dynasty: 1957-1986

Francois Duvalier comes to power and rules until his death until 1971. A former country doctor, he is known as "Papa Doc," or "President for Life." He maintains a tight grip on the population through the use of a paramilitary force known as the Tonton Macoutes, who terrorize the people at any sign of resistance. Political killings and arbitrary detentions affect thousands. Upon his death in 1971, Duvalier's son Jean-Claude, also known as "Baby Doc," succeeds him and carries out most of the same policies. Baby Doc is forced into exile in February 1986.

The Aristide Era: 1987-2004

The Late '80s

After Baby Doc flees, Haitians approve a new Constitution in March 1987. However, in the country's first attempt at democratic elections, hundreds are massacred at the polls by soldiers and Tonton Macoutes.

An army general, Prosper Avril, leads a coup d'etat and declares himself in charge in September 1988. General Avril suspends 37 articles of the new constitution and declares a state of siege. His rule is marked by political violence and human rights abuses. Right-wing death squads and the threat of military coups are the norm. A large wave of Haitians attempt to flee this political turmoil and violence, often in leaky boats headed for the United States and other nearby countries.

The '90s

Haiti's First Democratic Elections
1990—1991

Jean Bertrand Aristide, a young Roman Catholic priest, is elected president by more than two-thirds of the voters in a crowed election. However, he is overthrown by a military coup less than a year into his presidency.

An estimated 1,500 Haitians are killed by the army in the first weeks after the coup against President Aristide. "Boat people" from Haiti began to flee in large numbers to the United States and other neighboring countries. The United States and the Organization of American States declared a trade embargo against the military regime.

Haiti Ruled by Military Junta; Aristide Reinstated
1991—1994

During rule by a brutal military government, thousands are reported killed, tortured and raped. Thousands more attempt to flee to the U.S. in small boats. Most are intercepted by the U.S. Coast Guard, which sends them back to Haiti, where they are often killed. Artistide is reinstated in 1994, under pressure from the Clinton administration.

Rene Preval Elected, Serves His Full Term
1996—2000

In February 1996, at the end of his original 5-year term (which had been interrupted by the Junta), Aristide vacates the presidency. He is the first elected president in nearly 200 years of Haitian history to peacefully transfer power to a democratically-elected successor. Rene Preval, a former Prime Minister under Aristide before he was ousted in December 1991, is elected president. Preval becomes the first president to ever to serve out his term.

Aristide Second Term Thwarted; Preval Elected Again
2000 to present

Aristide wins the presidency again in 2000. After a period of political violence, in 2004 he is again ousted in a military coup. A two-year period of political instability and chaos ensues. More Haitians risk their lives attempting to flee to the U.S. Many are intercepted by the U.S. Coast Guard, and others are lost at sea. The ones who reach the U.S. are subjected to mandatory detention and expedited removal procedures.

In 2006, after two years of unelected government supervised by United Nations peacekeeping forces, Rene Preval is elected President.

The Earthquake: January 12, 2010

A devastating earthquake levels Port-au-Prince, Haiti's capital. It is estimated 300,000 people have lost their lives. More than a million are made homeless.

Treatment of Refugees

In the years following the departure of Baby Doc, military coups and brutal military rule are unfortunate features of Haitian political life. The number of Haitian immigrants who try to immigrate to the U.S.—both those seeking legal residency and refugees seeking political asylum—goes way up. The U.S Coast Guard intercepts most of these refugees, sometimes thousands of them in a single day. This reflects the U.S. government's policy of intercepting and returning Haitians without screening them to assess the validity of their claims for refugee status. It contrasts with U.S. policies toward Cuban refugees, who are allowed to stay here if they reach U.S. soil. Human rights groups criticize this policy as contrary to international law. (Since the earthquake in 2010 the U.S. has suspended removal procedures for Haitian detainees.)

© Knopf

COURAGE AND COMPASSION IN THE MIDST OF TRAGEDY

Brother, I'm Dying
By Edwidge Danticat
272 pages. $23.95. Alfred A. Knopf

REVIEWED BY KAELA BAZARD

Brother, I'm Dying, by Edwidge Danticat, is an outstanding memoir that will tear your heart to pieces and glue it back together again. Danticat is well known for her novels, but this is her first book about her own life. In the book, she expresses her love for the two men who raised her and presents a sorrowful image of the tragedies some Haitians experience in the U.S. and in Haiti.

Kaela reviews Brother I'm Dying, *an account by the writer Edwidge Danticat of growing up in Haiti and the United States, and the tragic death of her uncle while in the custody of U.S. immigration officials.*

The story begins on a hot morning in July 2004 when Danticat discovers that she is pregnant at the same time that she learns her father is dying of a lung disease. This news is soon followed by more tragedy, this time relating to Danticat's Uncle Joseph.

Danticat was only 2 when her father emigrated from Haiti to the U.S. Her mother followed when she was 4, leaving Danticat and her younger brother in the care of her Uncle Joseph and her Aunt Denise. Joseph Dantica (his name is spelled differently from Edwidge's) was an extraordinary man: a minister, a survivor of throat cancer, and a role model who touched the lives of his family and community profoundly. He raised Danticat, her younger brother, and many other children of relatives and friends. Danticat lived with Uncle Joseph until she was 12, then she and her brother joined their parents in the U.S.

Her uncle's neighborhood in Port-au-Prince (the capital of Haiti) was a beautiful place but was (and still is) a political war zone. For years, Uncle Joseph refused his younger brother's pleas to emigrate to the U.S. He felt too bonded to his church, his school, and his life in Haiti.

But in 2004, while his brother (Edwidge's father) was battling a life-threatening illness, Uncle Joseph had no choice but to let go of that bond and flee to the U.S. That's because Haiti's President, Jean-Bertrand Aristide, had been sent into exile and the country was becoming a true war zone. When some United Nations peacemakers shot at a local gang from the roof of Uncle Joseph's church, the gang members destroyed his church and threatened to murder him. Uncle Joseph managed to escape and fly to Miami. But as we read in *Brother, I'm Dying*, that only led him to a more horrible fate—he died in an immigrant detention center there.

As Danticat brought her baby girl, Mira, into the world, the splendor of new life was offset by her family's heartbreaking loss. As Danticat describes this experience, her words will leave you out of breath. She turns grave adversity into a story of acceptance, courage, and hope for a better future.

I am a Haitian immigrant myself, and Danticat's book left me speechless with mixed-up emotions. I came here in 2000 and knew that a lot of people were leaving Haiti in 2004 after the president left. But never did I think the country was in such a horrific situation that they were burning churches and schools. I was also shocked and angry at how the U.S. immigration officials treated an elderly man like Uncle Joseph, who was 81 when he died.

I'm amazed at Danticat's ability to write such a powerful memoir about something so personal and emotional. Writing that book took a lot of courage and an honest heart. I remember when I lived in Haiti, many journalists were killed for sharing their opinions and speaking the truth on political issues. *Brother, I'm Dying* opens a portal to many issues that I've rarely seen Haitian writers explore.

DANTICAT TURNS GRAVE ADVERSITY INTO A STORY OF ACCEPTANCE, COURAGE, AND HOPE.

I'm also happy that Danticat chose the career that she did. In my experience, most Haitian parents encourage their children to become doctors or nurses. Writers? Well, not so much. The fact that Danticat followed her dream to become a writer—and succeeded—inspires me to take my own writing to the next level.

I would recommend this book to everyone, especially teens who are going through a difficult time. It can give you courage to deal with grief and help you stand firm through times of hardship. To me, the message of Danticat's book is that when the unfairness of life cuts down the trunk of your family tree, your roots will make the tree rise again, for they are numerous, strong, and full of momentum.

Kaela graduated from high school and attended college.

THINK ABOUT IT

What stories do you know about your family's history, or your relatives' journey to the U.S.?

Kaela suggests that Brother, I'm Dying *is about hope and strength in the midst of unspeakable heartbreak. Have you ever struggled to find courage in the middle of great adversity? What happened?*

ABOUT VOODOO

Thanks to Hollywood and the popular media, the word voodoo* conjures up images of black magic, sorcery, zombies, and people sticking pins into "voodoo dolls." These popular misconceptions distort the important role voodoo plays in Haitian history, society, and culture.

Voodoo, as traditionally practiced in Haitian culture, was born when African slaves mixed their traditional religious beliefs and value systems with the Roman Catholicism of their European slave masters. It survives today as an important link between Africa and Haiti.

Haitians who practice voodoo do not call it by that name. They simply refer to their faith as "serving the spirits." The word voodoo is derived from the West African Fon language of Dahomey (the area that is now known as Benin and Togo) that was home to thousands of slaves who landed in Haiti, and it means spirit. In Haiti, it can also refer to a kind of religious dance and, in some areas, to a pantheon of spirits.

Serving a pantheon (group) of spirits, known as lwas or loas, is at the core of the faith. Most of these spirits originate in West and Central Africa. Some of them are of Haitian origin, which can include historical heroes and ancestors. Thus, the specific spirits that are worshipped can vary among families and regions.

Belief in the spirits, however, does not replace belief in a supreme God. The spirits are simply more accessible than the supreme God. They are closer to helping in daily lives, somewhat akin to Catholic saints. As such, the spirits are respected and honored through rituals in which food, drink, and other gifts are offered to them.

Voodoo borrows heavily from Catholicism because slave-masters forbade its practice. To avoid persecution, for example, slaves used Roman Catholic saints to stand-in for African spirits. But unlike the Catholic Church, voodoo does not have a central authority. Priests, called hougans, and priestesses, called manbos, serve to mediate between humans and spirits through divina-

---

*Voodoo is the popular spelling and is used in this book. Scholars tend to use vodou or vodoun, in part to differentiate the actual practices from the popular misconceptions.

tion and trance. These individuals often have extensive knowledge of herbs and can treat a variety of illnesses as healers of both the soul and the body.

Like all religions, voodoo provides a structure of beliefs that explain the mysteries of life and death and help believers address the challenges of surviving daily life. It is similar to other transplanted African traditions such as Candomblé, found in Brazil, and Santeria in Cuba. Some of the most powerful spirits are: Legba, Marassa, Loko, Danbala, Ezili, Kouzen Azaka, Ogou, Jean Petwo, and Bawon Samdi.

HOW YOU CAN HELP

The rebuilding of Haiti's homes, schools, and hospitals, and its political institutions, is going to take a decade or more. Haiti is a poor country, and donations make a big difference in its ability to recover. If you would like to help, we encourage you to make a donation through Partners in Health, which has a 20-year history of providing effective and efficient medical care and other services throughout Haiti.

Partners in Health
P.O. Box 845578
Boston, MA 02284-5578
(617) 432-5256
http://www.pih.org

There are many other organizations that have also done work in Haiti, including Wyclef Jean's Yéle Haiti (www.yele.org), World Vision (www.worldvision.org), and the Red Cross (www.redcross.org). If you have a favorite charity, look it up on the web to see if they currently are doing work in Haiti and need support for that work.

CREDITS

The stories in this book originally appeared in the following Youth Communication publications:

"Tomorrow Is Promised to No One," by Cassandra Charles, *New Youth Connections*, February/March 2010; "I May Not Look Haitian, But..." by Marsha Dupiton, *New Youth Connections*, March 2009; "My Mother Risked Her Life for Us," by Gerty Jean-Louis, *New Youth Connections*, May/June 1994; "A New World Full of Strangers," by Edwidge Danticat, *New Youth Connections*, September/October 1987; "Solitary Confinement in the 1st Grade," by Daniel Jean-Baptiste, *New Youth Connections*, December 1992; "I Found a Way to Make My New Country Home," by Kaela Bazard, *New Youth Connections*, April 2007; "A Goat Named Manush," by David Etienne, *New Youth Connections*, April 2008; "Dream Girl," by David Etienne, *New Youth Connections*, May/June 2008; "My Mother's Gift," by Raelle Charles, *New Youth Connections*, December 2006; "I Showed My Enemies, and Hurt My Friends Too," by Elie Elius, *New Youth Connections*, September/October 1998; "Stick With Your Own Kind?," by Cassandra Thadal, *New Youth Connections*, January/February 2004; "Fights in American Schools Freaked Me Out," by Sabrina Rencher, *New Youth Connections*, May/June 2001; "Dating, Black Magic, and Other Changes in America," by Claude Fravien, *New Youth Connections*, May 1989; "A Haitian-American Christmas: Cremace and Creole Theatre," by Edwidge Danticat, *New Youth Connections*, December 1984; "I Still Fear for My Family," *New Youth Connections*, December 2008; "I Wanted to Be Pretty and Popular," by Sabrina Rencher *New Youth Connections*, April 2001; "Moving to the Music," by Raelle Charles, *New Youth Connections*, November 2006; "Rewriting My Dream," by Marsha Dupiton, *New Youth Connections*, November 2008; "What Happened to My American Dream?" by Natalie Neptune, *New Youth Connections*, March 2005; "A Little Piece of Haiti," by Natalie Neptune, *New Youth Connections*, September/October 1997; "Haiti's Part in America's History," by Cassaundra Worrell, *New Youth Connections*, January/February 1988; "Courage and Compassion in the Midst of Tragedy (Book Review: Brother, I'm Dying)," by Kaela Bazard, *New Youth Connections*, April 2009.

ABOUT YOUTH COMMUNICATION

Youth Communication, founded in 1980, is a nonprofit youth development program located in New York City whose mission is to teach writing, journalism, and leadership skills, and to make youth voices heard as widely as possible. Each year, 100 public high school students write and illustrate Youth Communication's two award-winning teen magazines. The writers are a diverse group, including teens in foster care, recent immigrants, and low-income youth. Working with full-time professional editors, the writers may take several months to complete a single story. This process results in writing of uncommon depth and authenticity. The true stories in this anthology were written by teens in the Youth Communication writing program.

In addition to publishing magazines, Youth Communication has published more than 70 anthologies on topics teens consider most important, such as peer pressure, families, and improving their communities. Stories by teens at Youth Communication are also frequently reprinted in popular and professional magazines.

Youth Communication strives to serve three primary audiences: teen writers, teen readers, and educators.

• Writers: Writing for peers motivates teens to develop their literacy skills, meet deadlines, think critically about their experience, take individual responsibility, and work as a team to produce high-quality magazines.

• Readers: Teen readers report that reading their peers' stories makes them feel less isolated and more hopeful about the future. They also say that the stories give them information they can't get anywhere else and promote discussions with parents and other significant adults.

• Educators: Teachers and youth workers use Youth Communication publications to inspire reluctant readers and to broach difficult topics in safe and stimulating ways. They also report that reading our books and magazines shows them what's really important to teens, which helps them establish better relations with their students and clients.

Youth Communication ®
224 W. 29th St., 2nd fl.
New York, NY 10001
212-279-0708
www.youthcomm.org

ABOUT THE EDITORS

Dana K. Vincent was born in Haiti and came to the United States at age 10. She grew up in Brooklyn and wrote for Youth Communication while a student at Clara Barton High School. She is an alumna of Spelman College, the New School, and the Georgetown University Law Center. She has worked as a lawyer in both the public and private sector. She is due to start a clerkship with the Honorable Sterling Johnson, Jr., a senior United States District Judge for the Eastern District of New York.

Keith Hefner co-founded Youth Communication in 1980 and has directed it ever since. He is the recipient of the Luther P. Jackson Education Award from the New York Association of Black Journalists and a MacArthur Fellowship. He was also a Revson Fellow at Columbia University.

Laura Longhine is the editorial director at Youth Communication. She edited *Represent*, Youth Communication's magazine by and for youth in foster care, for three years, and has written for a variety of publications. She has a BA in English from Tufts University and an MS in Journalism from Columbia University.

WITHDRAWN

9 781935 552475